AMERICAN BARNS

and

COVERED BRIDGES

by

Eric Sloane

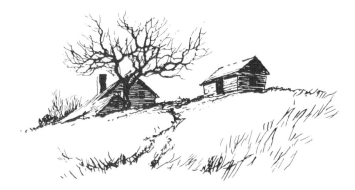

DOVER PUBLICATIONS, INC.
MINEOLA, NEW YORK

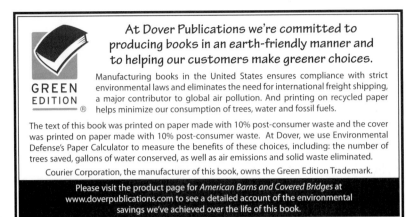
Copyright

Bibliographical Note

This Dover edition, first published in 2002, is a republication of the book originally published by Funk & Wagnalls, New York, in 1954.

Library of Congress Cataloging-in-Publication Data

Sloane, Eric.
    American barns and covered bridges / Eric Sloane. —Dover ed.
        p. cm.
    ISBN-13: 978-0-486-42561-0 (pbk.)
    ISBN-10: 0-486-42561-4 (pbk.)
        1. Barns—United States. 2. Covered bridges—United States. I. Title:

NA8201 .S6 2002
728'.95—dc21

                                                                    2002074185

Manufactured in the United States by Courier Corporation
42561405
www.doverpublications.com

Author's Note   *page 7*

THE WOOD   *page 11*

THE TOOLS   *page 30*

THE BARNS   *page 50*

THE BRIDGES   *page 80*

A Census of Covered Bridges   **Page 112**

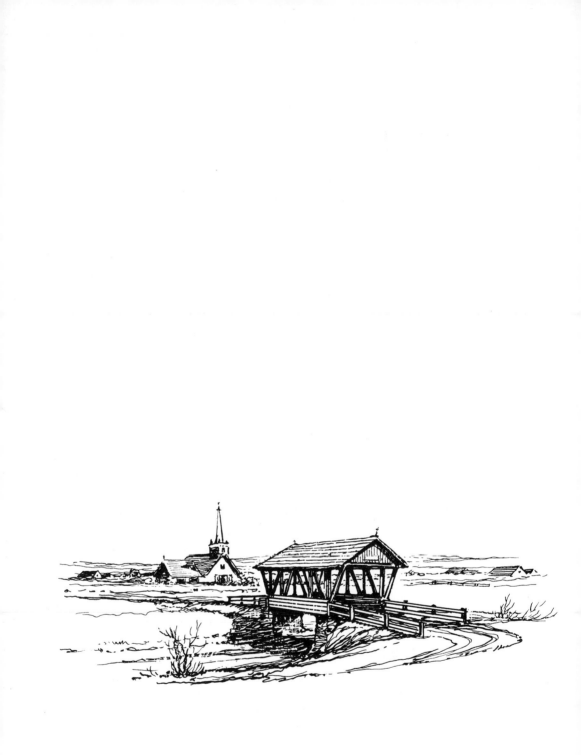

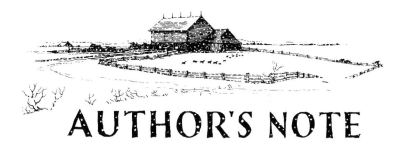

AUTHOR'S NOTE

THIS BOOK began one day when I was dismantling an old barn. The ironlike quality of the old wood and the cleanness of the adze cuts made me wonder what those times must have been like, and what sort of man the builder of this barn had been. For on lifting a timber from a part of the dry-wall, which had been plastered over on top and protected from two hundred years of weather by the covering of wood, I found the imprint of the builder's hand. Every callus and scar was there, and even the skin pores were visible. To me it was as though he had reached down across the years to greet me, and right then and there I knew I'd continue seeking to know better that first American, the Barn Builder.

As I sit now, drawing and writing amidst an array of long-disused tools and old almanacs and my sketches of rotting wooden structures, my children often confront me with the question, "What is an antique?" Anyone who has ever tried to explain a love for antique things to a child will understand my quandary. But one day my youngest answered the question when she said, "Is my teddy bear an antique?" Teddy Bear, I might explain, has one eye gone along with most of his fur which makes him related somewhat to my ancient and well-used barns and bridges. Teddy Bear certainly was an antique! He was a symbol of something past; but age had nothing to do with it and his condition was entirely beside the point. A love for antiques is not explained, it's something you acquire.

I'm not worried about my youngest. I think she might still have Teddy Bear when she is as old as I am; I think she will also be surrounded with the spiritual beauty and perhaps some of the tangible things that are the heritage of her forefathers. On the other hand, she might succumb to the modern habit of discarding old teddy bears, supplanting them with new ones of plastic. In any event, although there may well be not one ancient barn or original covered bridge left in America for her to see, there will still be this record.

Hand-hewn woods and barns are not confined to America, of course, but somehow the American pioneer gave to his craft something that has made his barn like no other barn in the world. The pioneer's love for wood and his skill in using it, together with the surviving examples of early American wooden architecture and artifacts, are fast disappearing. To revive an understanding and adoration for wood seems as hopeless as trying to bring back the horse and buggy. But to revive the eloquence of those times is indeed worth while. This book of sketches and comment is designed to lift the old barn and covered bridge out of the category of quaintness and the antique curiosity and to secure for them a rightful place in the story of architecture so that we may better see and feel the fine fabric of American development.

Things are never beautiful just because they are old. Let it become our duty to seek out and select the authentic beauty of the past and so keep it alive for the future. Goethe said it this way: "Whatever we come upon that is great, beautiful, significant, cannot be recollected. It must from the first be evolved from within us, be made to become a part of us, developed into a new and better self, and so, continuously created in us, live and operate as part of us. There is no Past that we can bring back by the longing for it, there is only an eternally new Now that builds and creates itself out of the elements of the Past as the Past withdraws."

So, rather than preserving things just because they are old or exulting in the fact that a Washington slept in its front bedchamber, one can take pride in the house that breathes the early American spirit by sheer dignity of form, purity of line, by a fine use of the right wood. Surely this is better than masquerading it in ancient costume by decorating it with antiques. The modern builder by the same means can borrow from colonial grace without resorting to patent nostalgia.

Those old structures were functional for reasons of life and death, whereas we wear our modern functional style too often as a uniform of distinction or as a decoration. There have always been fashions in architecture but the early American farmhouse style is an exception because it is never out of fashion. The farm and its barn buildings, in harmony with their setting, and simple in their Grecian plainness, do not seem subject to obsolescence. The Athenians built with marble, the Americans built with wood but the two architectural forms were founded on simplicity and—as with some ancient Greek ruins—I feel that I am in the presence of greatness when I happen upon a crumbling ruin of an early barn.

An architectural style is too often merely a criticism of some other style. The "revolt" trend in design reflects an unhealthy philosophy. When patriotism depends upon the hatred for another nation, or when one moves to the country because he hates the city or builds a traditional house because he hates the modern ranch-type, then there is snobbery in the making. The barn builder, in creating a new style, was being architecturally honest; he neither borrowed nor revolted against a foreign style, he was merely a serviceable carpenter creating a future. Which, by the way, is an inspiration for American thinking, architecturally and otherwise.

The great names of the American past have been well recorded but the country barn builder is anonymous. Those who would find the spirit of early America must look first in the country: in the city no one whistles yesterday's tunes. In the country the old tunes sound best; to those who can hear it, the song sung by old barns and wooden structures is precious music. It can be informative music too, for old houses speak as plainly as humans. An early barn or a hand-hewn bridge, though often regarded as a landmark or a curiosity, is better still a shrine. Beholding it is the closest thing to an intimate communion with the plain people who first kindled the American spirit and who evolved that architectural inheritance which has all but disappeared.

Sometimes echoes seem to be the loudest noises. I hope this book, like the sound of ax and adze across the countryside, will bring back some of the past and give a new importance to America's old barns and bridges and to all things that were once made only of wood.

I built those stalls and that shed there; I am barber, leech and doctor. I am a weaver, a shoemaker, farrier, wheelwright, farmer, gardener, and when it can't be helped, a soldier.
—FROM *Travels in the Confederation, 1783.*

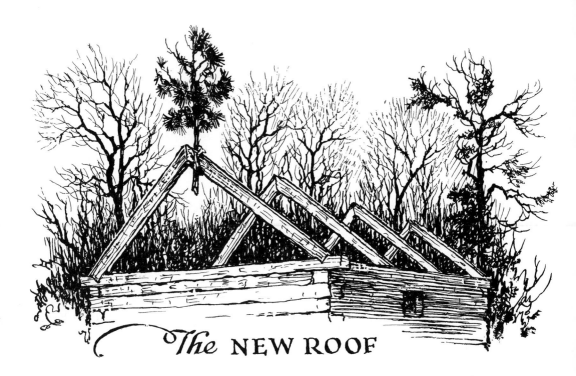

The NEW ROOF

~The~ WOOD

The log at the wood pile, the axe supported by it;
The sylvan hut, the vine over the doorway, the space cleared
for a garden,
The irregular tapping of rain down on the leaves, after the
storm is lull'd,
The wailing and moaning at intervals, the thought of the sea,
The thought of ships struck in the storm, and put on their
beam ends, and the cutting
away of masts;
The sentiment of the huge timbers of old fashion'd houses
and barns.
—WALT WHITMAN

THE FOUNDATIONS of the American nation were laid with the building of its first barns. The hewn rafters of the first Plymouth barn were put in place and, with a prayer of thanksgiving, a small tree was lashed to the peak as part of the ceremony. Builders still put that symbolic tree on the rooftree of a new house without any particular reverence for wood itself, but just for "the luck of the house." The great importance of trees in the forming of an American philosophy seems almost lost in this plastic age.

You can't cut down a group of trees without being impressed by the characters of their wood. Some woods will accept the ax cleanly, some cut stubbornly, others will bounce an ax away unless the differences are allowed for. Just as a child today knows the differences between aluminum and spring steel, the early American child knew the differences in the softwoods and the hardwoods. Children today can point out any automobile and tell its make, but two hundred years ago they could point out any wood or even smell it and call it by name. Without learning it in school or by book, it was perfectly natural for any American to know that black gum was for plowshares, oak for framing and pegs, apple for saw handles, chestnut for barrel hoops, cedar for pails, pine for kindling, and oak for heat. Even the plainest carpenter knew that a rocking chair needed at least four kinds of wood. Each wood did its specific job; there was pine for a soft seat, hickory for a springy back, walnut for strong legs, and oak for the fastening pegs. And any eighteenth-century farmer had the knack of making wooden hinges, locks, nails and spikes, hooks, plows, rakes; almost all his needs around the farm were satisfied with nothing more than a sharp tool and the right kind of wood.

Our forefathers were steeped in the romance and tradition of wood. The forest and its trees were part of their thinking and language. If a man were weak, strong, honest, or dishonest, he was likened to some kind of tree and although such a simile would not be very impressive today, it hit home then.

The old-timer interpreted man by likening humanity to the forest, saying: "There are warped and crooked trees that grow from poor soil. They just hold the soil together but they are neither beautiful nor useful and there are men just like that. There are trees like the dogwood that are just put on earth to be beautiful. There are fast-growing trees that crowd out everything but their own kind, that look like strong trees but are soft and weak inside. Some of their family are even poison to the touch and unfortunately there are men like that, attractive only from a distance. Then there are the tall hardwoods that become taller and stronger because of long, cold winters and high winds; broken limbs have left rough calluses along their trunks, but they stand out in the forest of trees like leaders. There are the soft, radiant woods which can be molded into useful things that become richer with age and smoother with usage; there are men like that too."

Asked to name something symbolic of America, we might first think of wheat, gold, silver, iron, or steel. Few of us would think of wood. Yet from the beginning, the greatest wealth of our country has been wood. Twenty years after their arrival, the Pilgrims were exporting American white pine as far as Madagascar in ships built of American trees. Scouts of "His Majesty's Woods" stalked through New England forests seeking suitable mast wood for Britain's Navy. Even as late as 1830, trees were seen with the King's "Broad Arrow" mark branding them as the property of England.

To think that the coming of iron eliminated some of the need for wood is wrong, for it was wood that made the Iron Age possible. Our greatest forest clearing was done to make charcoal which up until a century ago was the only fuel known for smelting iron. It might be argued that America's real growth came later with the steel railroads, but again wood enters the picture. One of the few things in America that has never changed with modern improvements is the railroad tie which is the same as it was when the first locomotive was made. Locomotives first used wood for fuel, but even today as the Twentieth Century flashes past at ninety miles an hour, it passes four thousand wood ties and a hundred wood telephone poles a minute. Stop now to think how much of the present American scene is composed of wood—books, newspapers, money, checks, bonds, documents, and deeds (even the page you are now reading was once a tree). Continue on with plastics, medicines, paints, houses, furniture, ships, and almost every conceivable necessity only to find in wood the source material. Even our coal and oil originated in ancient forests. America has been from the beginning a vast wood workshop.

The first settlers obtained sugar from maple trees; their soap came from fireplace ashes boiled with fat; charcoal went into their gunpowder; leather was tanned with oak bark and their medicine closet consisted of remedies derived entirely from the forest. Even colors for dyeing clothes came from the trees; there was butternut for brown, hickory bark for yellow, white maple for gray, sassafras bark for orange, and sumac for red. Almost all early American needs were filled by the wealth of the forests.

It seems strange that with all our modern methods, today's lumber is so very inferior to that used two hundred years ago. Even the best of modern kiln-dried wood cannot equal the keeping quality of wood as "prepared" by the early craftsmen. If you doubt this, try to buy an absolutely straight ruler today; hold any so-called straight-edged new piece of wood up to your eye and you will frequently find a curve that will increase with years. Yet some old houses have pine doors only a half inch thick by twenty-four inches wide that are as straight as the day they were cut, even without bracing. This was no accident, for the early settlers knew their wood. Their wood wisdom began from the moment the tree was cut. If cut at the right time, some insisted that lengthy "seasoning" was less important, often unnecessary. An old almanac states, "If you'd have your flatboards lay, hewe them out in March or Maye." During the "old moon of February" the New England woods rang with ax blows, for, according to belief, that was the right time for cutting timber that would stand forever straight and unwarped. It has even been suggested that the word "seasoned" as in "seasoned wood" has reference to wood having been cut during the proper season of the year. We are not in an age of folklore, but be it superstition or science, the results have certainly been interesting: the *New England*

Farmer says, "The moon has potential influence in the various parts of her orbits, that by cutting one tree three hours before the new moon and another of the same kind of tree six hours afterwards, a difference in the soundness of the timber would be noticed." "When the moon is new to full," reads an old almanac proverb, "timber fibers warp and pull." There were rules even for cutting firewood, for an entry for January 6, 1799, in an early Almanac advises, "At this quarter of the moon, cut fire wood to prevent it from snapping and throwing embers beyond the hearth."

Another proverb says "wood that lives with face away from sun, doesn't warp when sap has run." This suggests that wood cut from the north side of a tree (where the green moss is prevalent and where the sun shines the least) is less liable to warp from further dampness after milling. In the early days when pine flooring was cut, the log was first split in half. The northern half, according to custom, was kept for wide floorboards, while the southern side was quarter-sawed for lumber where warping might be less important.

It is quite true that almost every early builder had his own methods of seasoning and that each method was often so distinctive that one would contradict another. In all cases, the care and time taken to hew and turn the timbers by hand aided in the natural seasoning or drying of the wood. But the method used by the experts involved the presoaking with water; as logs were often moved from place to place by the simple means of floating in a stream or river, this alone might often have taken care of the soaking process. But let an early description in The *Builder's Handbook*, 1732, speak for the methods and the times of fine wood seasoning:

"There are some who keep their timber submerged in water to hinder the cleaving; this is good in fir, both for better stripping and seasoning; yea not only in fir but in other timber as well. Lay therefore your boards a fortnight in water (if running as in some mill-stream, the better) and there setting them upright in the sun and wind so it may pass freely through them, especially during the heats of summer which is the proper time for finishing buildings. Turn them daily. Thus treated, even newly sawn boards will season better than many years of dry seasoned methods. Let then the floorboards be tacked loosely for the first year and nailed for good and all the next year. Elm felled ever so green, for sudden use, if plunged for five days in salt water obtains admirable seasoning and may be immediately used. Water seasoning is not only a remedy against the worm but for its efficacy against warping and the distortions of timber. There are some who bury their timber in the earth, others in wheat. There are those who season by heating with fire, as for the scorching and hardening of piles. But for general seasoning and quick use, the soaking methods seem best."

Quarter-sawing was the practice of sawing boards so that the grain (when looking at the butt end of a board) runs as nearly at right angles with the width of the board as possible. Because warping is often caused by the grain "fighting against" a shape contrary to the grain's anatomy when the wood dries, it stands to reason that if you cut in harmony with the grain, you will then have less warping. Quarter-sawing is still being done, but the waste along with the necessity for huge logs and the resulting number of odd-sized widths makes quarter-sawing an expensive process. The dictionary will tell you that quarter-sawing is done to better "show the grain": how little were the settlers concerned about how the grain looked and how wrong the dictionary would have been two hundred years ago when quarter-sawing was done only to prevent warping! Actually many of the old buildings were built by plain farmers who were less concerned with carpentry than you might suppose and good wood took over where their poor carpentry left off. To say, "Ah, they built houses right in those days," does not explain why the house remarked about is found to contain all sorts of odd and erratic measurements that would be frowned upon today. Few rooms were actually square, ceilings were seldom the same height at the opposite side of the room and "random width" floorboards were more accidental than intentional. So what? Generally speaking, the materials were better than the carpentry, but the buildings were sounder, more pleasing, and more lasting.

In the beginning, well-seasoned timber was the result of simple convenience rather than of special effort. Dry wood burns better, cuts better, and weighs less, so it became perfectly natural to allow all wood to dry well before using it for any purpose. An old farmer's calendar reads: "It is said that a cord of green wood weighs about fifty-six hundred weight; a cord of dry, thirty-eight hundred weight. If then a farmer consumes thirty cords yearly and sleds it green, he sleds twenty-seven tons of water more than his neighbor who sleds it dry. Besides, if this wood is burned green, it requires wood enough in addition, to evaporate twenty-seven tons of water in order to obtain the same amount of heat. Using only dry wood is a saving of labor and expense."

Good seasoning of wood, which simply means proper drying, is regarded as a lost art or a matter of using more time than we have to spare now. Actually, the pioneer had much less time than we have today: he was in a hurry to get his barn or his house built, for the cold of winter would not wait. It is strange that, even with today's conveniences or so-called time-savers, we seem to have less than time permits. Good workmanship and the hand-made things of wood that have endured without rotting or warping are too often passed off with a wave of the hand and a remark about "people having more time to do things in the old days." How much less time they

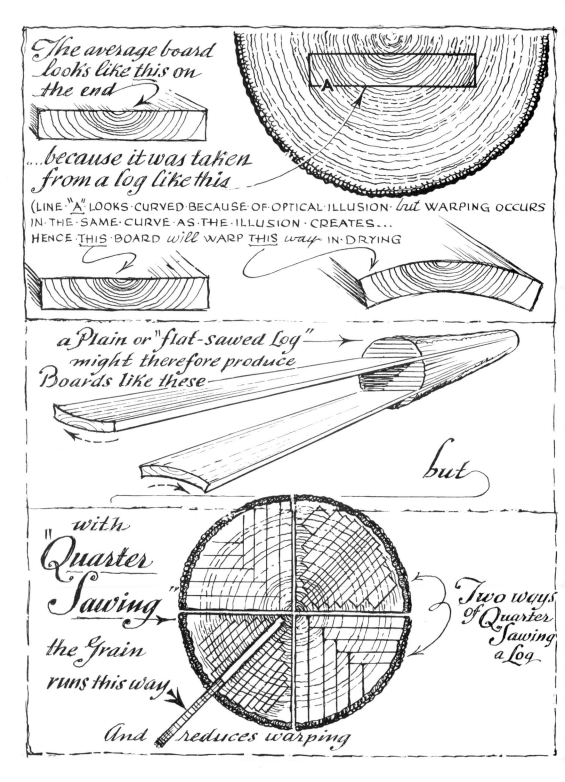

The average board looks like this on the end

...because it was taken from a log like this

A

(LINE "A" LOOKS CURVED BECAUSE OF OPTICAL ILLUSION *but* WARPING OCCURS IN THE SAME CURVE AS THE ILLUSION CREATES... HENCE THIS BOARD *will* WARP THIS *way* IN DRYING

a Plain or "flat-sawed Log" might therefore produce Boards like these

but

with "Quarter Sawing" the Grain runs this way

And reduces warping

Two ways of Quarter Sawing a Log

16

had is realized by remembering that the workday of a union carpenter now is not much longer than the chore time needed by the early backwoods carpenter before he even started his day of "work." Add to this the fact that there were only candles then, and when the sun went down the craftsman's day was over.

The time "saved" by mechanically-dried wood today is really lost many times over by having to paint-preserve it or even to discard or replace it a few years later. Furthermore, properly seasoned wood will harden with age and soft woods will often assume the properties of hardwood. It was the custom of match factories to buy large quantities of well-dried pine and so, when one factory heard that the old Ninth Street Bridge in Pittsburgh was being taken down, it put in a bid to buy all the white pine it contained. The factory regretted this move for the pine could not be made into matches; even an ax could not slice the once soft pine which had now become as tough as red gum or green sycamore.

The first settlers learned tree wisdom from the Indians. Cutting lower bark away for shelter and canoes, the Indians found that this operation killed most trees. So the art of girdling or killing a tree by cutting away the bark began. The usual practice was to girdle the trees that were on land to be farmed later. When the trees died, the summer sun reached through the naked branches and a garden could be hastily created even in the forest: later, as time permitted, the dried trees were felled and utilized as partly seasoned timber. A few years back, when America's chestnut trees were struck with a blight, several lumber firms bought quantities of the "dead" wood and found that the timber had seasoned nicely before it was even felled, making ideal warp-proof building material.

While girdled trees and quartered timbers were drying in the sun, there were always farm jobs, land clearing, rock wall building, and the thousand chores of everyday life to contend with. Hewing and chipping, cutting and setting, might take three months, although the actual raising of a barn often was accomplished in a single day. It was fortunate that the colonial builder was also a woodsman. What carpenter today knows his wood when it stands in the forest? But it all went together in those days, the clearing of land for raising food, the hewing of lumber, and the building of houses. The interrupted carpentry work probably gave some extra time for the wood to dry out.

In 1798, Isaac Weld of Dublin was in America making sketches and reports of the American way as seen through the eyes of a foreigner. Impressed by an ability to clear land, he commented that "these people have an unconquerable aversion to trees—to them the sight of a wheat field or a cabbage garden conveys pleasure far greater than the most romantic woodland views." Earlier, in his *Travels Through the States of North America, 1797*, he wrote: "The fact of the matter is, that from the face of the country being entirely overspread with trees, the eyes of the people become satiated with them. The ground cannot be tilled nor can the inhabitants support themselves until they are removed; they are looked upon as a nuisance and the man who can cut down the most of them and have the fields about the house clear of them, is looked upon as the most industrious citizen and the one who is making the most improvements in the country." Isaac was only twenty-one then and he was speaking as a fashionable member of the Irish gentry at a time when it was chic to wax romantic about the wonders of nature. He was "showing off" and being far too critical. If he had ridden through America seventy-five years earlier he would have known why the settlers were so proud of their clearings. Like Isaac, even now it is hard for us to realize the dangers of those early days, when pioneers, moving into the heart of a strange country with wild animals and savages at the door, valued the farm clearing as a safety "moat" between their homeplaces and the forest. But even a hundred years before Isaac's visit there were American conservationists; for back in 1681 William Penn decreed that one acre in every five be left in trees.

The clearing of land gave rise to one of the first industries in America. To clear the land much wood had to be burned and burned wood left ashes containing potash which was used for making soap. "Soap ashes" was the chief wealth of some of the first American settlements. Large quantities of wood ashes were tamped down in huge vats with holes underneath; water was poured in from the top and the residue contained lye salts which were boiled down and chiseled out of the pots when cool.

Large tree roots were found too difficult to burn and almost impossible to dispose of, so the "root fence" was devised. A stretch of roots with their tentacles turned upward made a menacing enclosure for cattle or for protection from Indian attack. There are still many root-fences in the north country and some in the far west. Generally speaking, however, the root-

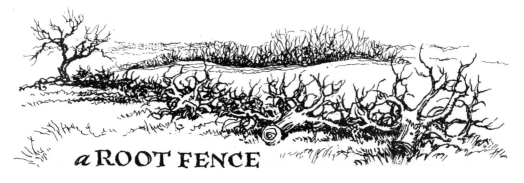

a ROOT FENCE

fence was temporary, especially in New England where fence-consciousness became almost a form of fanaticism. An early copy of the *Christian Almanac* from Boston reads, "be tolerant of thy neighbor and be not jealous of the condition of his fences." A sound fence or stone wall became the rural sign-post of a good farm and any farmer insisted that he could glance at one and tell the character of the man who built it.

Those who have wondered why fences or walls in the city have a menacing appearance that is entirely absent in the country, should remember that in the city fences keep things out while in the country fences keep things in. There is an almost human friendliness in the early stone walls of New England that makes you wonder what the people were like who built them. A hundred years ago a "no trespassing" sign in the country would be the signal of downright unfriendliness but "no hunting" was always permissible. Some of the old walls had an upraised flat rock here and there bearing the "no hunting" legend in white paint. Typical of New England friendliness is a sign done on a barn, at the farmer's insistence, by the sign-painter who did the patent-medicine advertisement on the opposite side. It read, "If you can't stop, wave as you go by."

Actually the walls are merely stones cleared from the fields and piled neatly to one side. But they happen to make fine enclosures. As a Connecticut farmer remarked, "They're better than wood fences because when they fall down you still have material to put them back again."

The Oriental philosophy of contemplation involves forsaking all work; the European does his meditating while relaxing from work, but the American seems to think things out best while working. So the stone walls of New England may be thought of as monuments to the thoughts that occurred while they were being built, for those were the days of great decision and profound planning. The thoughts one thinks while sawing a tree or making a stone wall are surprising. It is almost as if the mind becomes ashamed of the work the body is doing and starts doing a little "showing off" by itself. Lincoln said he did some of his deepest thinking while splitting rails. The plain farmer of two hundred years ago was weaving the fabric of a new nation and although there are no marble statues to his patriotism now, there are still his stone walls.

In the beginning no farmer attacked his land clearing alone but when the trees were felled and ready to be piled aside or burned, the whole country-side gathered for the "log-rolling." When they left, most of the heavy work had been done and only the smaller stone moving was left for the farmer and his oxen. Each participant was entitled to take home his load of special wood—young maple limbs for baking fuel, alder for gunpowder charcoal or whatever he needed most. Ashes in those days were valuable for what they

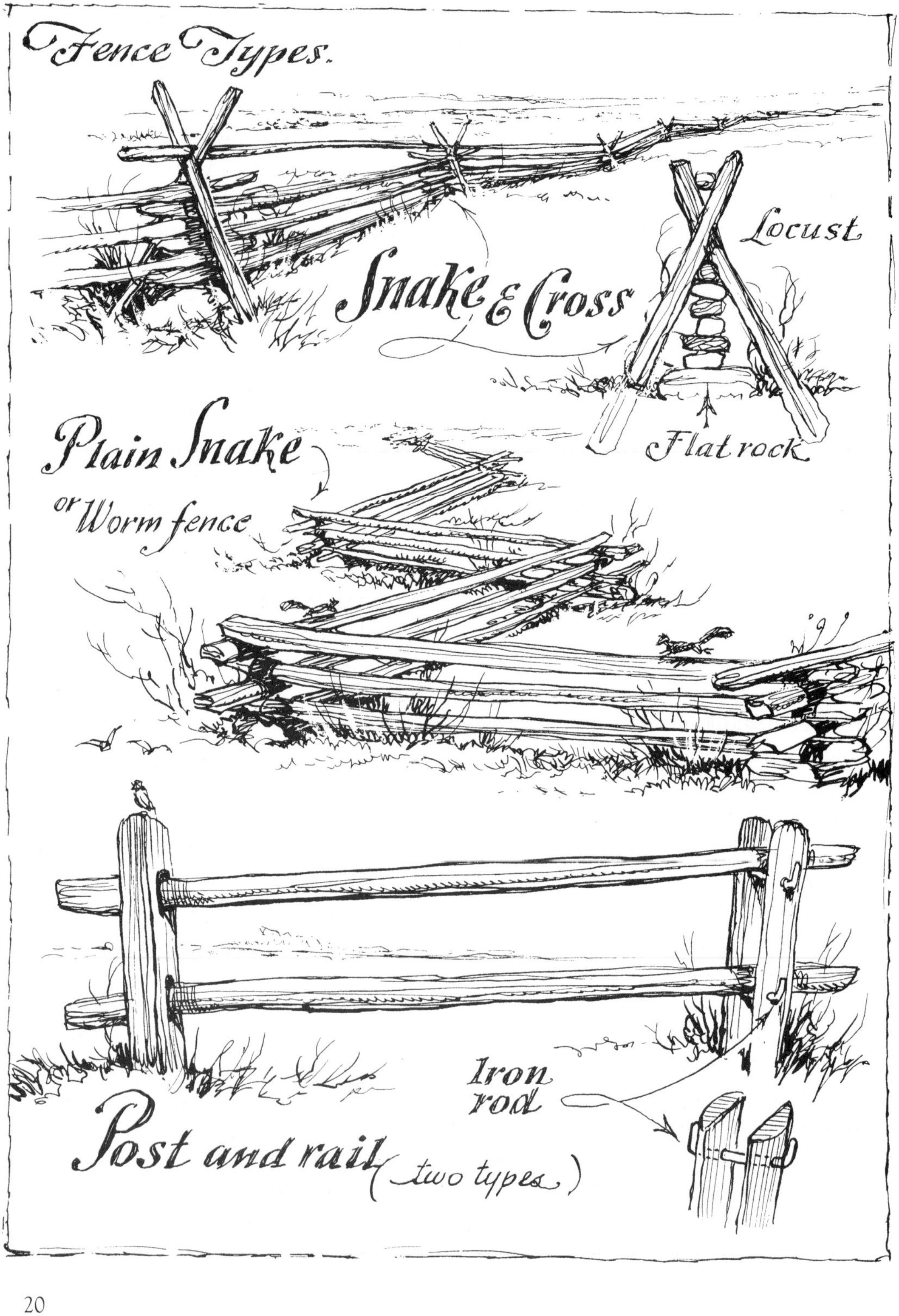

Fence Types.

Snake & Cross

Locust

Flat rock

Plain Snake
or Worm fence

Post and rail (two types.)

Iron rod

contained and also what they did by way of preserving and insulating. Baking in the Dutch ovens was only possible by the even heat of clean ash; cooked meats were kept preserved within the insulating confines of maple and hickory ashes; the first wall insulation was a mixture of ashes and hay; bake-oven and fireplace ashes were not thrown away but kept till spring to use as fertilizer in the garden. Fifty years ago ashes from the kitchen stove were still being used for scouring dishes and cleaning knives. Every farm made its own soap from ashes at least once during the year. Near the barn there was a "leach barrel" filled with several layers of straw, lime, and ashes in that order; rain water was poured in daily from the top and what came out through a hole in the bottom was lye for soap. Six bushels of ashes plus twenty-four pounds of grease made one barrel of soap.

Another farm industry was the making of charcoal. Today we think of charcoal as being just something to cook and flavor the steaks with. Actually nothing has less flavor than charcoal which is tasteless. The settlers flavored their smoked meats with corncobs and hickory bark and not with charcoal. Charcoal does give much heat with little smoke and it is, therefore, an ideal fuel. Charcoal is wood that has been heated under cover, leaving just enough air to burn off the gases. What is left is almost pure carbon. Anyone old enough to remember the charcoal tablets which once were so widely used as a tooth whitener and as an aid for indigestion will recall how tasteless the stuff was.

Only a little over a century ago, charcoal was the basic industrial fuel for smelting iron. Each iron furnace drew its fuel from the surrounding hills and, although few of us realize it, the Iron Age did most to strip America of its early forests. One iron furnace would clear an average of two thousand acres of woodland annually for the production of charcoal and there were many hundreds of such furnaces. The J. and J. Rogers Company of Au Sable Forks averaged seven thousand acres of woodland each year.

The denser hardwoods such as beech, birch, maple, and oak were ideal for charcoal making and their wood was cut into four-foot lengths. The sticks were piled on end to form a hemispherical mound about ten feet high and twenty-five feet in diameter. This was covered with a flexible hood of ferns, hay, and sod, then fired from the top down through a hole in the middle. The slightest flow of air could cause an explosion that ruined days of labor nursing the slow manufacture of the charcoal. The work was, therefore, a twenty-four-hour-day job and the charcoal maker usually slept alongside his oven. Black and strange-looking from his unusual and lonely occupation, the charcoal maker was a colorful nineteenth century character of which little has been recorded. The simple life called for no mastery of the English language and as it was an existence not unlike that of mountain

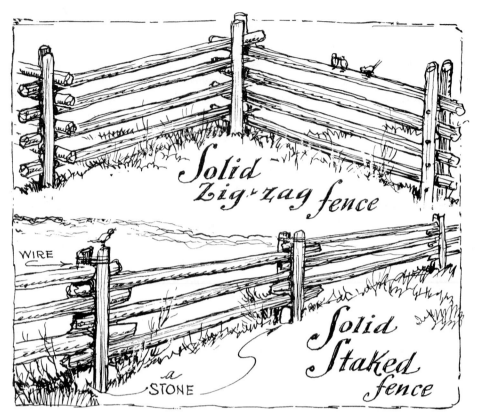

Solid Zig-zag fence

WIRE

a STONE

Solid Staked fence

farming or sheepherding, many Europeans, particularly Russian and Swiss, came over to partake in the new America iron bonanza and became charcoal burners. The communities that grew up around the charcoal and iron industries were very much like the western towns that were to come later with the gold rush. A war was on and iron was the great necessity of the day. In Connecticut, the town of Salisbury became one of the cornerstones of the structure of the Continental Army; guns, anchors, chains, and field pieces of every sort were manufactured there. The anchor of the *Constitution* was forged at nearby Riga; fittings and chains for the entire fleet were forged there and for a while the Salisbury pits were putting out over thirty thousand tons of metal a year. In 1778, the famous Sterling Iron Works began a rush order to make a chain for stretching across the Hudson to keep the British fleet from going up the river. It is said that the complete chain, weighing 180 tons and each link being about four feet long, was finished in six weeks at a cost of four hundred thousand dollars. The wood burned into charcoal to smelt ore for that one chain probably leveled a small forest. Such towns became the little Pittsburghs of New England until something happened overnight. The Bessemer process and the use of coke was invented. Charcoal was a doomed industry.

After twenty years of trying to make a living from the ravaged forests and the petered-out charcoal deposits, the charcoal clan became hill squatters in sad little cabins, a hopeless and stranded population. Living on woodchuck and small game, most of them died of malnutrition but a few struggled on with their solitary charcoal pits. The infrequent visit to town was usually an event, for living in rattlesnake country, the latter-day charcoal men were addicted to the use of what they called "rattlesnake medicine," or moonshine whiskey. But the visits to town became fewer and fewer until finally the charcoal-wood wagons returned to the hills never to appear again and the clans of mountain colliers were soon forgotten. What remained were the commercial pits nearer town and the charcoal made there was used for medicine, polish, fertilizer, and gunpowder.

Another extensive use for firewood was in the lime kiln which every farmer owned or had access to. The kilns were usually built by "lime men" who were experts at kiln construction. The lime men traveled about the country making kilns for farmers, sometimes selling housewares and iron stoves as a sideline. The little stoves that are now sold in antique shops as toy stoves are often working models of real stoves which the agent brought to the housewife for demonstration. Stoves, incidentally, were about the only things that the farmer could not build for himself. Almost everything in the early days was made on the farm and every farmhouse had its own smokehouse, forge, and woodworking barn. The farmer was a jack-of-all-trades and there were few specialists.

But the increasing uses of wood called for European specialists and the New World always had room for those woodcraftsmen who were known as coopers. Although we never hear about it now, no ship would put out of port without having at least one good cooper. Several of the crew of the *Mayflower* were coopers. It is interesting to note that John Alden was accepted in the already-filled crew roster only because of his training as a cooper. The coopers of America were to be important people because dishes, hardware, containers for solid food and liquids, almost everything used as a container, had to be made of wood. In this trade of wood specialists there was the wet cooper—also known as a tight cooper—who made staved casks and barrels for all kinds of liquids; he was an expert with oak wood. The dry (or slack) cooper made barrels for sugar, flour, and meal. He was expert with maple, elm, and chestnut. Small tubs, butter churns, bowls, plates, and boxes were made by the white cooper who was expert with birch, beech, maple, and pine. All these things were called "treenware" from the early plural of trees. The cooper's shop was usually the busiest in town but during summer when his apprentice could take over, he took to the backroads, his wagon stocked with staves, hoops, and assorted treenware to call on his customers. A visit from the traveling cooper often lasted the day for there was always an abundance of wooden utensils to be repaired.

When the first coopers came over from England, they found much to be learned from the American Indian. The Indian had already devised an adze, almost exactly like the European shipwright's adze though the blade was made of flint. By burning fires in a log and adzing out the charred parts, the Indians made huge wooden canoes. This does not sound impressive to us, but it must have been so to the early settlers, for some of the canoes made by the Indians from one log were much longer than the boats in which the settlers themselves had come to America. It is quite natural that all early treenware should be influenced by American Indian design. This is most noticeable in treenware handles which were frequently designed in the Indian manner.

Sometime during visits to antique shops one comes across a wooden bowl of unusual hardness and extreme luster, having a wavy "bird's-eye maple" quality to the wood grain. That is a "burl" wood bowl, copied directly from similar bowls used by the Indians before the white man arrived. A burl is an abnormal wartlike growth occurring on the trunks of trees and is of hard and irregular grain. By cutting this lump from the tree and burning out the inside, an unusually beautiful and serviceable wooden eating-bowl was made that had no tendency to crack along the grain.

The use of particular woods to suit each need was the cooper's special art; chapters could be written about how each wood reacts to different liquids and how the cooper took this all into consideration, knowing how loose or tight to fasten each kind of wood and how to match up the right woods to make a perfect container. Consider the sap bucket. The hoops were hickory saplings with the bark left on; the staves were of maple to blend with the sap; the spiles or spouts which the sap ran through were sumac or basswood with the pith burned out by a heated wire; wooden pegs for fastening the hoops were made of birch.

At one time the only sugar available in America was from the maple tree and up until the 1800's many farms still derived sweetening from nothing but maple trees and the honey-bee. An average tree yields from five to fifteen pounds of sugar. "Sugarin' time" in the past must have been a wonderful event. The maple grove was usually a mile or so away from the farmhouse and in the middle of the grove there would be a sugar cabin where the whole family and perhaps a few hands would live the while sugaring went on. The children watched and emptied the sap buckets into large wooden sap barrels which were then collected on sugar sleds drawn by oxen. The fires were kept going for three days and three nights; the whole affair had a festive mood more of a frolic than the hard work it really was.

in The Cooperage trade there was

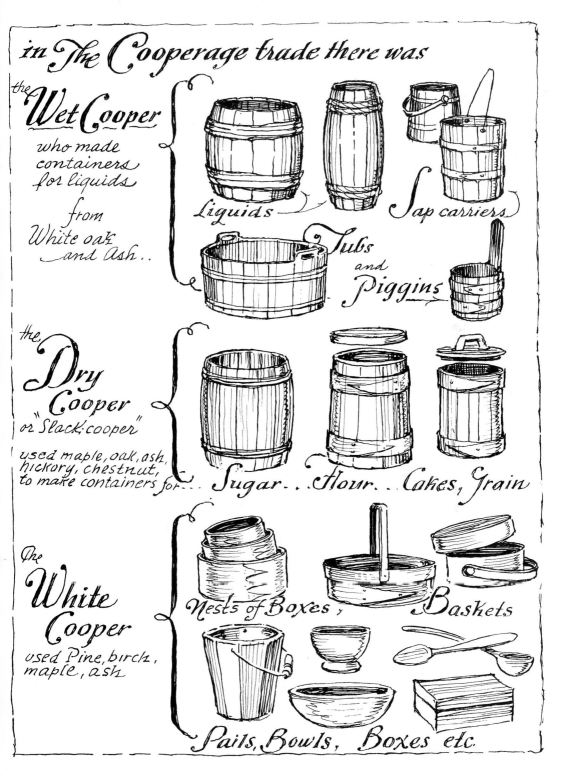

the Wet Cooper
who made containers for liquids
from White oak and Ash..

Liquids

Sap carriers

Tubs and Piggins

the Dry Cooper or "Slack cooper"
used maple, oak, ash, hickory, chestnut, to make containers for...

Sugar... Flour.. Cakes, Grain

The White Cooper
used Pine, birch, maple, ash

Nests of Boxes,

Baskets

Pails, Bowls, Boxes etc.

The first run of sap made a pure white sugar which was hardened into cakes and, usually placed in the attic out of the children's reach, reserved for special cakemaking. Each run of sap became darker and made different qualities of "soft sugar," syrup, or maple-molasses and each product needed its special kind of treenware to hold it. For example, hard sugar takes on the flavor of whatever material it is enclosed in, so pine and similar odorous woods were avoided. Wherever there was a grove of sugar maples, there was work for the cooper.

In later years when coopers were scarce, it became the common thing to buy five-gallon tins from paint companies at wholesale rates and use them for storing syrups. There is a tale about a New York man who bought an old Vermont barn to remodel; he found ten five-gallon tins in the loft labeled "Fine Varnish" and upon opening them he found the contents to be still smooth and clear. But it wasn't until the handyman had scraped two rooms and finished them off that he realized he had been using maple syrup to "varnish" the floor.

At one time apple butter and apple cider were as evident at the dinner table as bread and butter are now. No tree was more important than the apple tree which offered raw fruit, vinegar for cooking and preserving, butter and drink, and wood for special tools. The use of apple wood for fuel was banned in several states and out of reverence for the many things apple trees have to offer, farmers still consider it unlucky to cut down old apple trees or sell the wood. Some of the toll-takers of the old covered bridges considered it unlucky to take money for apple-laden wagons on their way to the cider press. So it was the custom to have a basket of fruit ready beside the driver as payment for their way across the bridge.

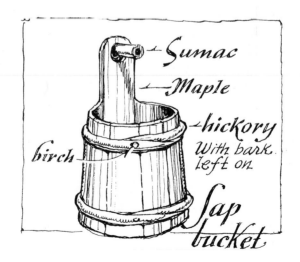

CEDAR was used as fence posts by all farmers because of its resistance to rot. Coffins were also made of cedar. There were cedar coopers who specialized in making tubs and pails. In Pennsylvania, cedar was used for making chests, which resulted in the present day "moth-proof" cedar closet.

CHESTNUT was first used for its bark which was cut in large squares and used as shingles on early barn roofs. Having an irregular wavy grain, its warp resistance, when properly seasoned, makes for fine wide flooring and for heavy cooperage.

HICKORY was used first by the Indians for an oily liquor which was pressed from pounded hickory nuts, and called "pawhiccorri," whence comes the name hickory. A few of the larger masts of early sailing vessels were made of hickory. The "summer beam" in early barns and houses was often hewn from one hickory tree; this beam was the horizontal beam taking the main burden of the whole structure and its name was originally "sumpter beam," so called from the sumpter or burden horse. The young hickory limbs, with bark usually left on, were used as barrel hoops. In the spring when the sap was running and the wood was, therefore, more porous, loads of hickory shoots and hickory strips were weighted and sunk in a pond to soak until ready for use. The Indians used hickory for basket splints and the settler soon learned to copy their technique, even improving upon it later by using steam instead of slow soaking. The Shakers became expert in using hickory splint for making chair bottoms, baskets, and sieves.

PINE was once considered as the emblem for America. More uses for pine were found than with any other wood. Light in weight, pine does not decay easily even when wet and it found its way into all kinds of early furniture, floors, and outside walls. Because the trees grew so straight and the wood was so well suited and light, America traded ship and mast pine for everything from Haitian sugar to African slaves. Many distant countries thought for a while that pine was the only thing growing in America. Tar taken from pitch pine was an important "first industry" and pitch-pine splinters were used as tapers for matches. Pitch-pine knots were collected and stored in barns to be used as emergency torches for out-of-doors lighting and night-time hunting. Pine was the standard covering for both barns and bridges.

BIRCH was rated second among the hardwoods. It was a mainstay with the white cooper and it made perfect material for both lye-ash and charcoal. Both tanning-oil and wine were made from birch sap by the Indians and later by the settlers.

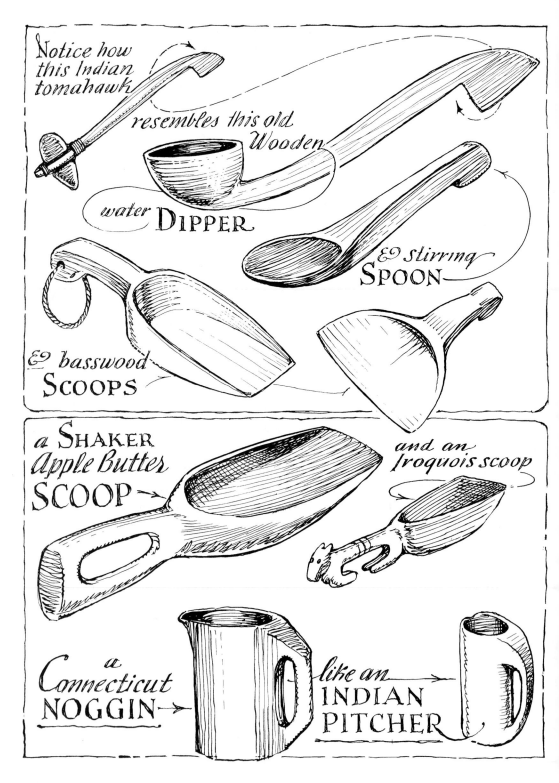

Notice how this Indian tomahawk

resembles this old Wooden

water DIPPER

& stirring SPOON

& basswood SCOOPS

a SHAKER Apple Butter SCOOP →

and an Iroquois scoop

a Connecticut NOGGIN →

like an INDIAN PITCHER →

28

Oak was the heaviest native wood and chosen first for framing barns and houses. Having no odor and bending easily, it was used by the wet cooper for barrel staves. Treenails or "trunnels" were made of oak. Because it was important in those days for fireplace wood to last throughout the night and also not to throw sparks, an oak log was always reserved for bedtime firelighting.

Spruce was abundant in the north and it was used in framing barns and in building bridges. Because it was the lightest yet strongest wood, spruce was reserved for long spans and bridge arches.

Ash has much of the quality of oak and, being a fast growing tree, it was considered a cash crop for the early farmer who sold the young ash trees for splint and barrel-hoop material. Many barns are framed entirely with ash although the fastening pins were always of oak.

These were the woods that made America a rich place. Richness to the European was something created so it was difficult for those across the sea to regard the New World as having wealth or culture of its own. As the European was a connoisseur of wine and perfume, the American took to his heart the aroma of good wood and the richness of pioneer life. To this day, few Americans find anything more invigorating than the smell of burning leaves, hickory-smoked hams, coffee on the stove, or the fragrance of pine. Who but an American would name an after-shave lotion "old spice," "pine chips," "sportsman," or "bayberry"?

No matter how "modernized" we are, somewhere out of the past will come a remembrance of wood, perhaps the crinkling of oak leaves in an autumn wind, perhaps the smell of a certain Christmas tree or of an old chunk of apple wood ending its life in your fireplace—and we share with the first settlers a reverence for wood.

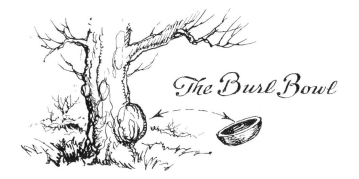

The Burl Bowl

ℭ𝒽𝑒 T O O L S

The Carpenter who builds a good House to defend us from
Wind and Weather, is far more serviceable than the curious
Carver who employs his art to please his Fancy. . . .
—FROM A Pamphlet of 1719

THE FIRST TOOL to be devised by man was the ax. But it met its greatest
test in America. The ax has had more to do with the building of our country
than any other tool. Within twenty years after the first settlement, the ax
had improved to the design we still use today. The settler used his ax to
a great degree of efficiency, from felling a tree to sharpening a twig of wood
in penknife fashion. He could hold the axhead in the palm of his hand and
smooth wood as we do now with a plane. He marked the handle with nicks
at every inch for measuring timber, and, by striking the axhead with a maul,
he had an improvised chisel.

Hidden out of the way in many old barns may still be found those
flat axhandle-shaped pieces of wood that were patterns for the making of
new handles. Their lines are simple, graceful, subtle, serviceable. Although
all axhandles look alike to the uninitiated, each man knew well the curves
and proportions of his own ax. They were as individual as his fingerprints,
as identifying as his signature. Once in ancient times, a murder was solved
by tracing the murder ax to the axhandle pattern in the murderer's barn.

The metal end of a tool is a cold and heartless thing, but the wooden
handle seems to assume something of the user's character. Whether it is
imagination or tradition, the good carpenter knows well the almost human
capacity of wood to "fight back" against pressure and its ability to improve
with age. Why a well-played violin or a correctly used tool is better for its
age is impossible to explain scientifically, but wood has that quality. The
handle, according to carpenters, is what has the "heft" or "feel" of a fine tool.

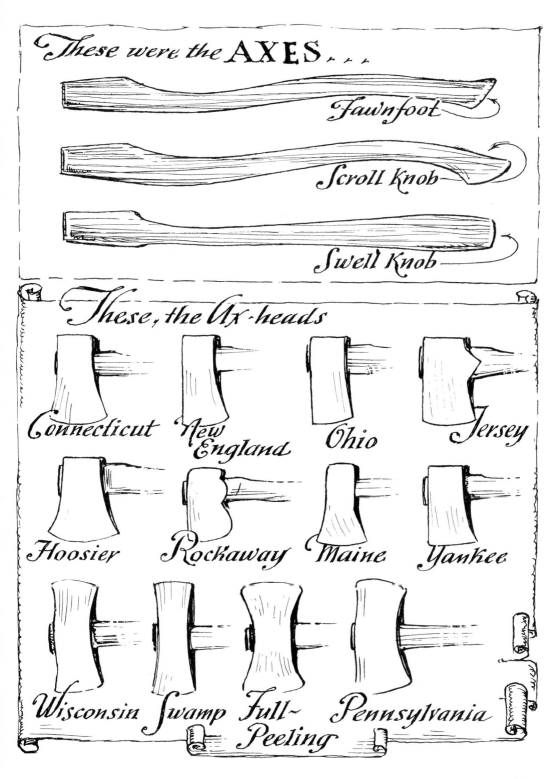

These were the AXES . . .

Fawnfoot

Scroll Knob

Swell Knob

These, the Ax-heads

Connecticut   New England   Ohio   Jersey

Hoosier   Rockaway   Maine   Yankee

Wisconsin   Swamp   Full-Peeling   Pennsylvania

The story of early American tools is more one of adoption than invention, because almost all woodworking tools had been invented in ancient times and had changed little since the time of the Romans. The chisel, for example, has never changed nor has the way of using it changed. Some people gush over the chiseled numbers at the joints of old barn timbers, saying, "See—they are done in Roman numerals, the way our forefathers printed." Yet when they mark their own modern screens and windows to match, those same people use Roman numerals too, because they are the only numerals that a straight-edged chisel can make.

The first ax brought over from England was heavy and it had a battle-ax appearance. But as the ax became more important and the axman more proficient in its use, a subtle variety in design evolved.

There were two kinds of American axes, the pole-ax and the double-bit ax: the pole-ax has a flat head and the double-bit ax two cutting blades. The axheads are as different in design as the axhandles, but, whereas the handle identified the man, the axhead told where he came from. Certain axheads were typical of Pennsylvania, Ohio, Michigan, Jersey, and so on.

Long before the time of the so-called Americana that we see in the average antique shop, all hardware and tools were made in the farmer's forge barn, which was a small house near the barn with a stone forge and chimney in it. Very often you will notice a toolshed with vestiges of a chimney and wonder why the farmer might have wanted fire or heat in such a place. When hard-

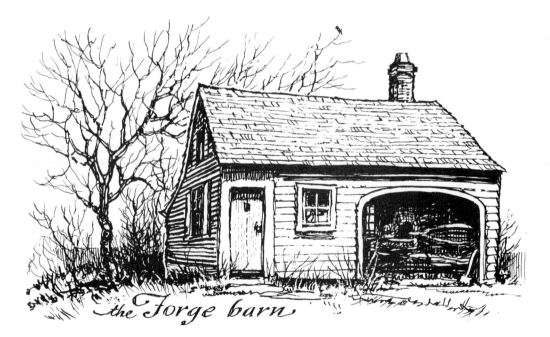

the forge barn

32

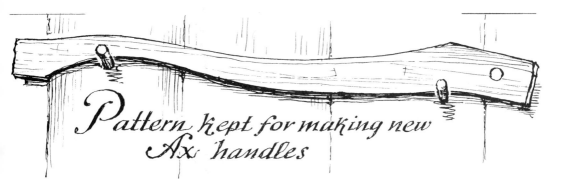

Pattern kept for making new Ax handles

ware became available without the usual British tax on it and tools could be made at the nearest blacksmith, the farmer's forge was usually dismantled and the forge barn became just a toolshed. But the fact that the earliest tools were hand-made at home and were skilfully used somewhat explains the very clean adzemarks and sharp mortise cuts that are often seen in the old hand-hewn barn beams. Many of the private forge barns had bellows over six feet long and were made from the hide of a complete moose or deer.

Spikes and nails were fashioned by hand in the forge barn until 1796, when a nail cutting-and-heading machine was devised and patented by G. Chandlee. Nails at one time were so expensive and in such demand that it was customary for the owner to burn down an abandoned building in order to recover his nails. In 1645 the colonial authorities in Virginia offered to pay the owner of an abandoned building the worth of its nails if he would not resort to burning the structure.

Symbolic of the Yankee carpenter, who is a fanatic about letting no one use his tools but himself, was a sign found in an old forge barn. "Using your neighbor's tools," it reads, "is like wearing his clothes." An old-timer who always made his own tools was once given one of those newfangled iron-handled hammers. "It's a fine tool," he said, "but it ain't a hammer. It don't sound like a hammer and it don't feel like a hammer. It's a fine tool but it ain't no hammer."

"Watching an axman," an early letter to England reads, "is like watching magic. These men of the woods sleep with their axes under their beds at night and every minute of the day they are swinging their blades with such sure strokes that they can just look at a tree and know how many strokes will fell it." A little later, a surveyor in New Hampshire tells how ". . . the axmen were identified from the surveyors by their type of headgear; bowlers are the standard headgear of the gentleman surveyor, while stocking caps are that of the axmen. The axmen go ahead as fast as one can manage to walk behind them, clearing the way as a ballet dancer might brush aside parlor chairs out of the way of his dance. Their axes are unbelievably small but they seem to cut twice as fast as anything that we have ever seen."

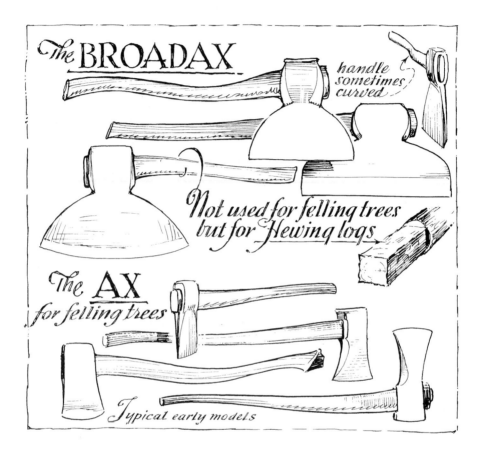

Although most people think that the early American broadax was used for cutting down trees, this short-handled monster was more a "carpenter-shop tool" than a woodsman's. Straight from the Middle Ages and weighing close to ten pounds, the broadax had one purpose and that was to make already felled, rough logs into serviceable building timbers; the process was called hewing. Here even the dictionary often goes wrong for, if you were to say that you "hewed a tree down" as some dictionaries say is correct for "felling a tree," your language to a seventeenth century person would be strange and incorrect. "The ax that fells a tree," goes an ancient proverb, "has not the wisdom of the broadax that hews the timber."

Each hewer had his own method of using a broadax. As it was beveled on only one side and the handle was often curved to "hug" the log that was being worked on, there were both right- and left-handed broadaxes. The general method of hewing was to go down the rounded top of a felled log with deep notches; then, with the beveled edge of the broadax up, the wood between each notch was hacked out. This went on until the rounded surface became flat; when four sides had been done, the result was a square beam.

A similar hewing instrument, but used for smaller logs, was the adze. All adze heads had square eyes or openings upon which the head slid. There were as many adze styles and combinations of handles as there were users. Because the adze was used on a timber that the hewer straddled, and the blade swept past between his legs, few old-timers went long without serious scars on both legs. The Indians had adzes of their own but they were flint blades and without a long handle. The Indian adze was really a knife-like scoop and, before using it, the wood to be hollowed out was usually softened by burning. During Indian raids, the settlers' adzes were sought for making into tomahawks and many of the so-called "Indian war hatchets" displayed at museums throughout the country are really remodeled adzes stolen from the whites. From the drawing it may be seen that adze handles were unusually graceful, also that the heads are loose and not anchored on by an inserted wedge as in the case of the hammer and ax. The mattock and grubbing hoe of today are really earth-digging versions of the adze. The adze, as it used to be, still exists in the shipbuilding business.

Shingles were not cut; they were split or cleaved, or "rived" and the instrument used for making them was called a froe. It was one of the few tools that could be used sitting down, so Grandpa of a hundred years ago enjoyed riving shingles in the toolshed when there was nothing else to do; there was usually a large overstock of shingles on hand for roof repairs. A good dry piece of pine, cedar, or oak was used, and the froe was placed blade down and with the grain, on a cross section of a chunk of log. With one blow of a maul or a wooden mallet, the froe would split thin sections or "shakes" from the chunk. Making a smooth and nearly finished piece of wood by just one blow is a fascinating operation and one can understand why Grandpa enjoyed his "riving" only second best to whittlin' or crackin' hickory nuts. There is nothing attractive about a froe. The blade isn't even sharp and the handle is just any old piece of round wood that was handy. The art of "riving" was a trick that needed no skill so there was no pride or dignity reflected in the design or construction of the tool. Even the maul that went with it lacked in grace; it was just a round "hunk of wood with a handle on it."

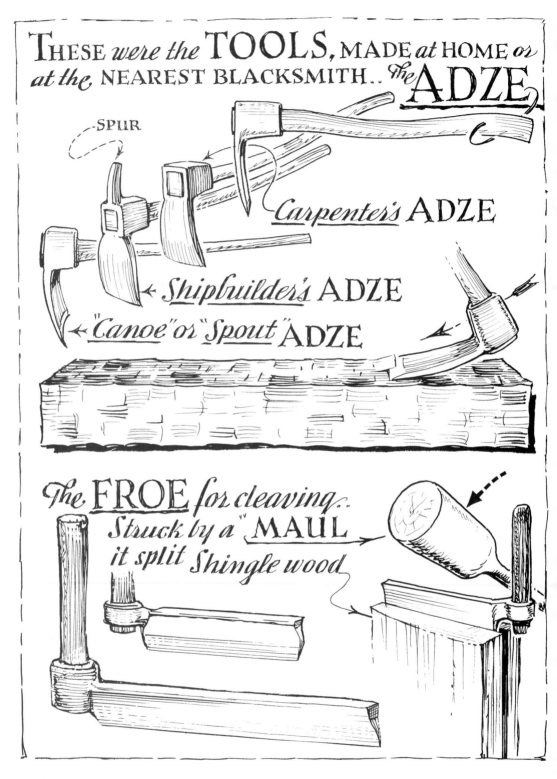

THESE *were the* TOOLS, MADE *at* HOME *or at the* NEAREST BLACKSMITH... *The* ADZE

SPUR

Carpenter's ADZE

← *Shipbuilder's* ADZE

← *"Canoe" or "Spout"* ADZE

The FROE *for cleaving..*
Struck by a " MAUL
it split Shingle wood

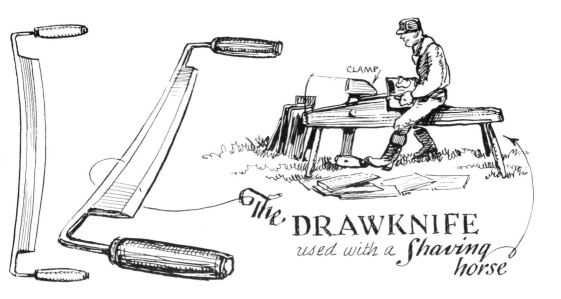

The DRAWKNIFE
used with a **Shaving** *horse*

Shingles usually needed a little trimming and smoothing, and that's where the shaving horse came in. Another sit-down job, the shingle was held in place by a "dumbhead" or clamp which was operated by the foot. A green branch to pull the clamp back when the foot was released, added to the automatic action of the shaving horse. Shaving was done with a nicely balanced blade, that was drawn toward the worker with two handles, called a drawknife. The drawknife was also used for peeling strips of wood such as the splint wood used in heavy baskets and as the hoops for barrels.

These five were the tools of the past that the barn-builder forged in his own forge. The ax, the broadax, the adze, the drawknife, and the froe were born ages ago, but the refinements given to them by the first settlers

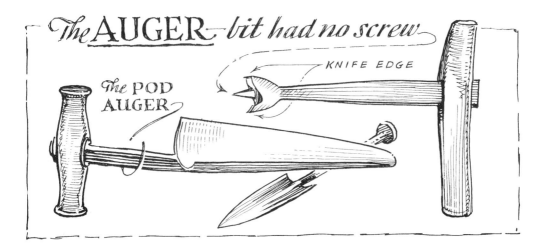

The AUGER *bit had no screw*

KNIFE EDGE

The POD AUGER

allow them to be described as American. The other tools of those days were very much like modern tools except for a fuller use of wood and some refinement of design. The auger looked like a giant corkscrew except for the absence of the pointed screw on the end; in its place was a sharp point and two cutting knives edged at an angle. The woodscrew was a late development, for until between 1840 and 1850, woodscrews had flat ends instead of sharp points.

A list of the old tools might sound little different from a modern list. In 1622, England gave some written advice for adventurers to the New World, telling them of the many cases where families had left the homeland poorly equipped, suffering privation and death as a result. "Those leaving for Virginia," this declaration read, "must provide themselves with the following tools for a family of six:

> 4 hoes, 3 shovels and 2 spades
> 2 broadaxes, 5 felling axes
> 2 steel hand-saws, 2 two-hand saws
> 1 whip-saw with file and set
> 2 augers, 6 chisels
> 2 pickaxes, one grindstone
> Nails of all sorts.

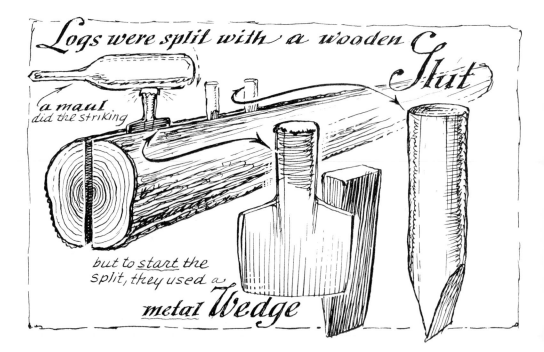

Logs were split with a wooden Glut — a maul did the striking — but to start the split, they used a metal Wedge

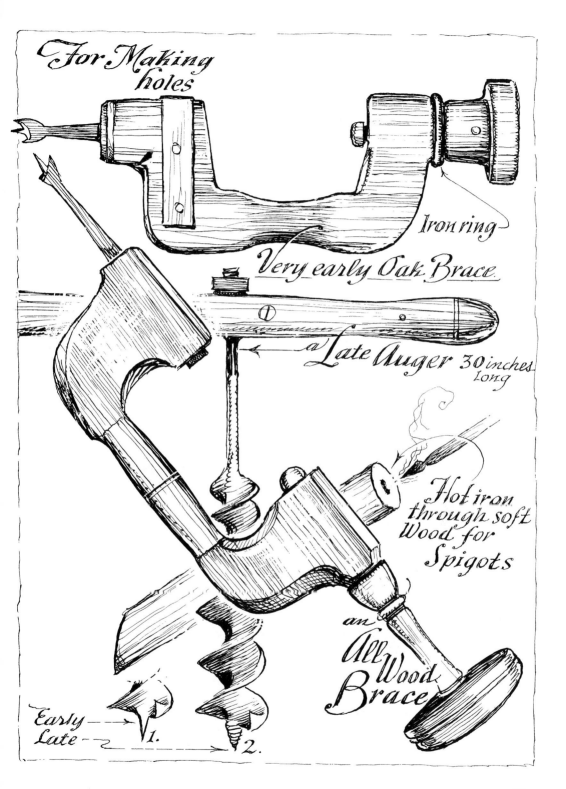

For Making holes

Iron ring

Very early Oak Brace.

a Late Auger 30 inches long

Hot iron through soft Wood for Spigots

an All Wood Brace

Early
Late

1.

2.

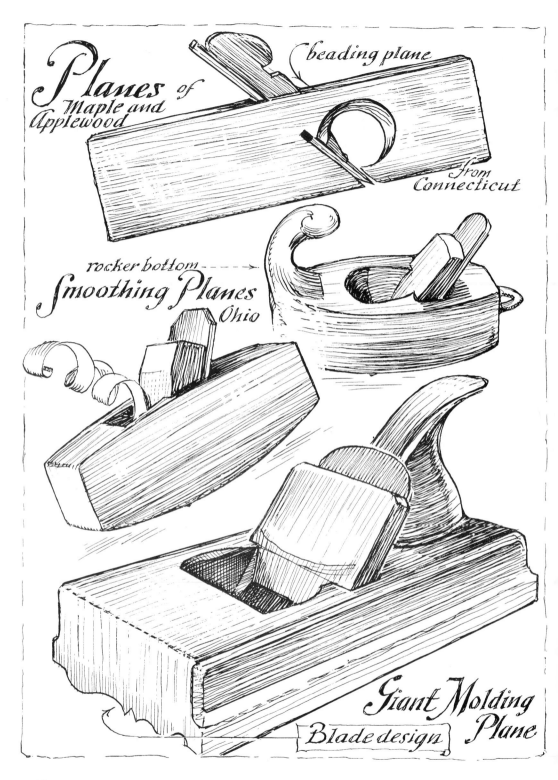

Planes of Maple and Applewood

beading plane

from Connecticut

rocker bottom

Smoothing Planes Ohio

Giant Molding Plane

Blade design

40

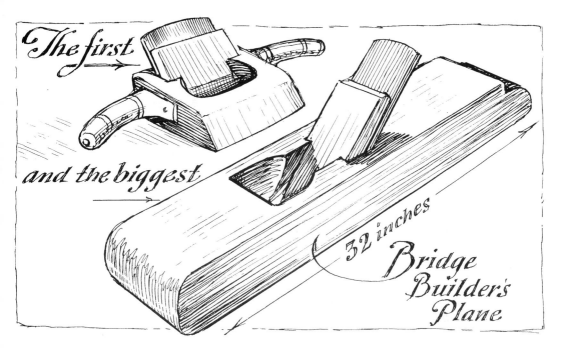

The first →

and the biggest →

32 inches

Bridge Builder's Plane

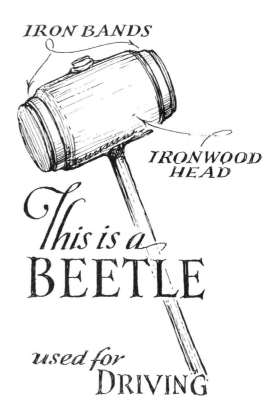

IRON BANDS

IRONWOOD HEAD

This is a
BEETLE

used for
DRIVING

If you happen to find a few flat-cut wooden wedges in your own old barn, perhaps they are gluts, which is just an unpleasant-sounding word that means wooden wedges for splitting logs. It seems incredible that plain wooden pegs can split a big log in two, but if you know your rail-splitting, that's the way to do it. The settlers had few steel wedges to spare and they found that just one steel wedge may be used to start a split and if followed up by plain wooden gluts, the job could be done as well as if all steel wedges were used. Gluts were about a foot long, fashioned of specially hard wood, while green and often hardened further by heating slowly over hot coals. Gluts were driven in by sledge-hammers called beetles—hammers with hardwood heads that were bound together with bands of iron. Beetles were generally used for driving stakes into the ground but often took the place of a maul. The maul and beetle were made of ironwood, black walnut, or oak, and both tools were used for driving trunnels into place.

The plane was a later development, first used like a drawknife that was pushed away instead of being pulled toward you in drawknife fashion.

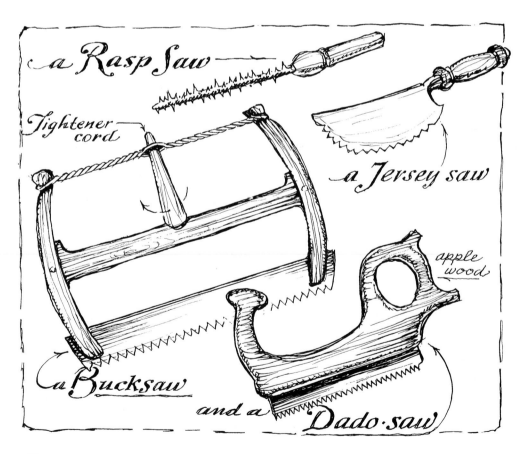

42

Some of the first planes were actually known as push-knives. The plane had an adjustable blade which was held in place by a hardwood wedge. Planes were used for beading, beveling, molding, and many other uses besides just smoothing a board, so each carpenter had a great assortment of planes on hand. He often had so many of them that they were kept piled in barrels. Early American tools have not found a popular market in the antique shops and many of the old wooden planes in their original barrels have found their way to the junk yard or have been burned for firewood although their cutting surface still does a perfect job. But the restored villages with their woodworking shops have revived interest in old tools and have already saved many a fine old wooden plane from the woodbox.

Some of the "bridge planes" were a yard long and were almost too heavy for the average person to manipulate. In fact, many of the old tools seem massive to the point of being unusable by the average carpenter of today, and it is assumed that the carpenter of yesteryear was a superman in size and strength. Some of them were just that, to be sure, for the times

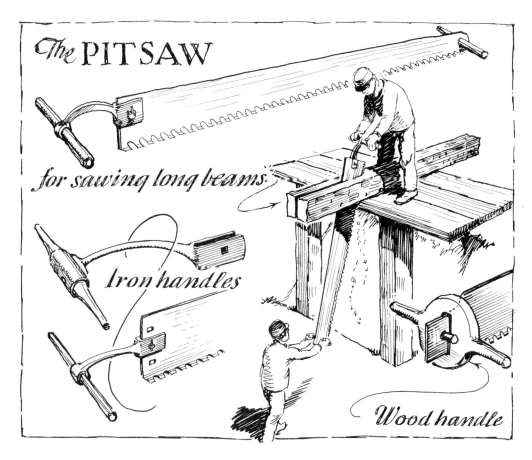

The PITSAW

for sawing long beams

Iron handles

Wood handle

were rugged and every man's morning chores would be pretty stiff setting-up exercise for any man today. But the fact is that many tools like many carpenters were also small. Tools were made for the hand of the individual carpenter, some small, some large. Perhaps most of the smaller tools were destroyed while the larger ones survived. The proof of an apprentice's manhood, however, was said to be when he could plane a huge shaving up overhead and down behind his back and it was the custom in those days for the apprentice to print his name on this first gigantic planing with the word carpenter after it for all to see.

The first organized carpenters were the sawyers who specialized in sawing wood. When the two-man pit-saw business started, the sawyers rose up to let their annoyance be known, seeking protection for "members of the sawyer trade losing their just work in the community." But when the water-driven sawmill was established, the sawyers became violent and even banded together to burn the sawmills. This "union" of sawyers seems to be the first closely protected trade which went to many of the present-day labor-union extremes. The saw-sharpener, for example, kept his trade a secret and operated in a closed room with a bell handy. When the saw was sharpened, he rang the bell; before that, no one was entitled to watch him.

The pit-saw was a very long two-man saw designed to be used up and down instead of horizontally. Sometimes one man stood on a raised platform but the convenience of not lifting a log soon led to a pit with one man down below. The saw pit and the pit-saw became a necessary part of the barn building. As many barns were built into the side of a hill, the saw pit was ready-made and sawing went on within the barn foundation. Seeking an improvement on the pit-saw so as to keep its great length from "whipping," it was stretched taut in a frame or sash and this became the sash saw.

The sash saw went directly into the water-powered sawmill, with the sash and saw sliding up and down in a frame exactly like the mechanism of a present-day window; the whole contraption was operated by a water wheel and an actuating crank handle. Probably the first American sawmill was devised as early as 1630 for many have been mentioned as being in Delaware and New York State at around that time, but the earliest positive date concerns the one at Berwick, Maine, in 1632. A gang saw or series of saws set in one sash was devised a few years later in Virginia.

The sawmill was one of the busiest places in town. Where there was no town near a sawmill, houses and shops soon appeared, and many an American town owes its existence to an original sawmill. The wood that went to the sawmill was either bought outright by the sawmill operator or was left by a farmer who paid for the cutting. Payment in the old days

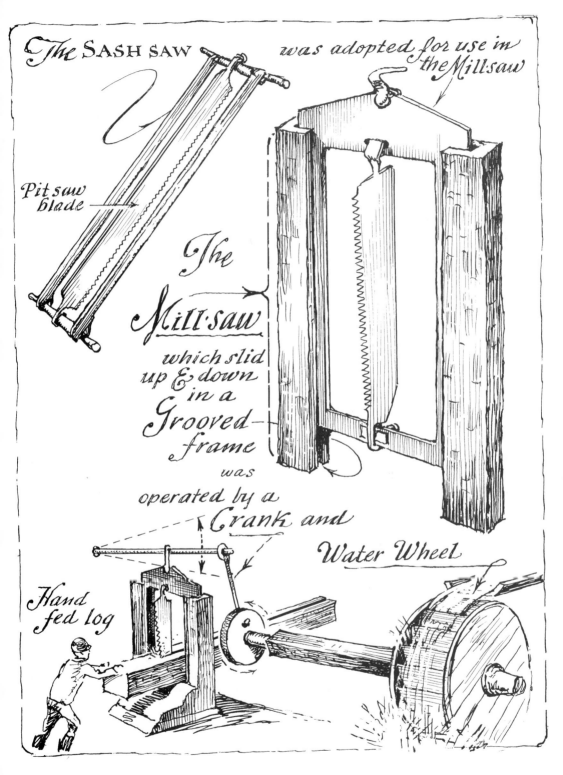

The SASH SAW was adopted for use in the Mill-saw

Pit saw blade

The Mill-saw

which slid up & down in a Grooved-frame

was operated by a Crank and

Water Wheel

Hand fed log

was never in cash but in wood (either standing or cut), butter, cheese, grain, or "what have you." So the sawmill operator often had to set up a shop to sell his barterings, and this established a trading base which expanded into warehouses, shops, and finally a trading community or village. There are so many towns named Millville, Millwood, Milford, Mills, Millington, Milltown, and so on, that the Post Office finds its biggest headache connected with the towns that grew up around these ancient mills.

Around the sawmill operator was an aura of importance that had many reasons for being. Because wood was often the only cash crop that the farmers could depend upon, the sawmill operator was often their town banker. When new roads were built and bridges erected, they always converged toward the mill to which the heavy loads of wood both cut and uncut traveled. The very river that actuated his saws was also the means of floating logs from distant places. Economically speaking, the sawmill operator of a hundred years ago was sitting pretty with America's first mass-production tool. The barn builder, the sawmill operator, and the bridge builder were closely allied. The simple trusses of the first bridges were tried out in barns and mills earlier, so, whereas the average carpenter

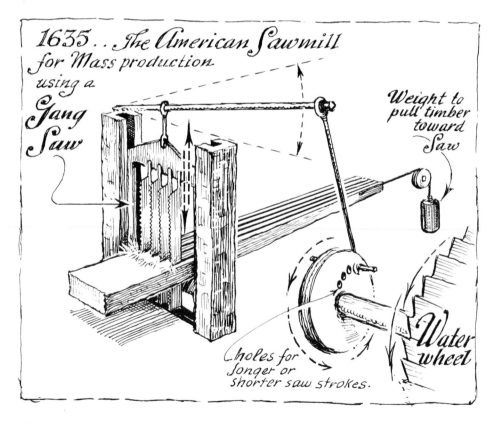

1635 ... The American Sawmill for Mass production using a Gang Saw

Weight to pull timber toward Saw

holes for longer or shorter saw strokes.

Water wheel

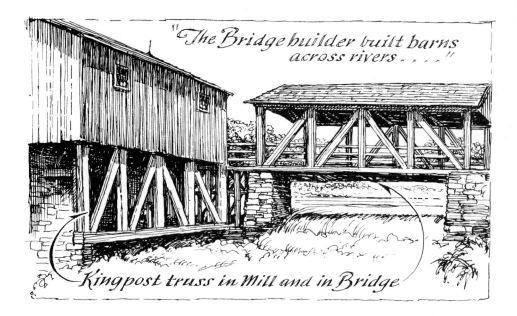

"The Bridge builder built barns across rivers . . . ."

Kingpost truss in Mill and in Bridge

of today would not feel qualified to build a bridge, for the barn-builder it was simple. He just put out over water the same sort of structure he had been making on land.

In 1820 the circular saw was introduced by the Shakers who are reputed to have taken the idea from the ratchet wheel of a clock. Because the circular saw did its cutting continuously instead of by the slow up-and-down or intermittent method, the process of sawing was speeded up tremendously. Sawmills that used a sash saw and were cutting one hundred feet of lumber a day during the last part of the eighteenth century, replaced the sash saw with a circular saw that cut fifteen hundred feet a day.

Although one does not ordinarily think of the sled as a tool, to the barn builder and the bridge builder too, the sled was a necessary tool. Not the sleds that dashing horses pull in Currier and Ives prints, but the heavy timber sleds drawn by oxen or sometimes the sledges without runners that just slide their burden from one place to another. To lift a one-ton stone into a wagon would be impossible, but to roll it by leverage onto a flat sledge only a few inches high was all in a day's work. Even if it could be got onto a wagon, the wheels would sink into farmland soil and then even oxen couldn't move it. But with a sledge or a sled, heavy weights could be slid over hard ground and soft, through mud or snow, during all times of the year.

Most people might think that hauling heavy loads would be most difficult in winter, but in the olden times the winter was reserved for just that thing. Sled runners will compress soft snow into hard ice and runners

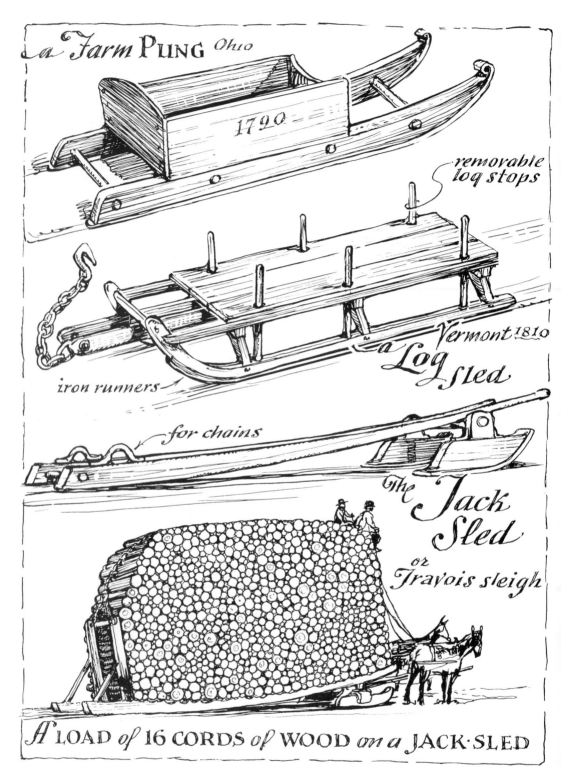

a Farm PUNG Ohio

1790

removable
log stops

iron runners

a Log Sled Vermont 1810

for chains

The Jack Sled
or
Travois sleigh

A LOAD of 16 CORDS of WOOD on a JACK·SLED

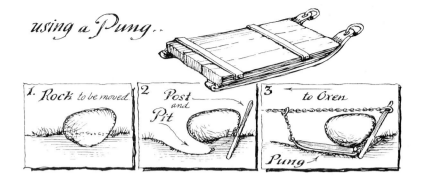

using a Pung...

1. *Rock to be moved*
2. *Post and Pit*
3. *to Oxen* — *Pung*

will slide easily over the ice with weights that oxen could not move by wheels on a dirt road. The greatest loads of wood have been pulled in this manner. The sixteen cords of wood shown in the drawing is no exaggeration and was traced from a photograph published in the *New York State Conservationist*. This is by no means a record, for a team of oxen can pull a heavier load.

Frequently one will see at the outer doorstep of a small farmhouse a flat stone as big as five feet by eight feet square, weighing over a ton, and wonder how it got there. The answer was leverage, oxen, the sliding action of ice during the winter, and a lot of hard work. But the sledge, or pung as it was called, was the tool used. Originally the word was tom-pung from which our toboggan was corrupted. It seemed to be the habit of calling each kind of sled by a nickname for there was the "Tom" pung, the "Jack" sled, and the "Bob" sled. One would move rocks with a Tom, carry wood with a Jack, and move light loads with a Bob.

Generally speaking, it is remarkable that with so few tools, the old barns were built as beautifully as they were. But when it is realized that log cabins were and still are being built with nothing but one tool, an ax, the necessity of many tools diminishes in comparison to the back-breaking labor that went into barn-building.

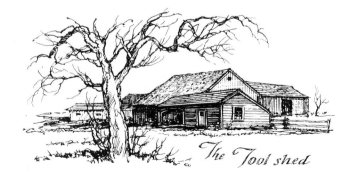

The Tool shed

𝒯𝒽𝑒 B A R N S

It is pretty to behold our backsettlements where the barns are as large as palaces, while the owners live in log huts; a sign of thrifty farming.

—Lewis Evans, 1753

In the beginning, the American barn was without glass windows or metal hardware because of the very heavy tax imposed by the Crown. Doors swung on hickory hinges and the nails were made of oak pegs. The inner silk bark of white pine was used as paper to make windows and huge wooden treenails or "trunnels" were used to fasten the beams together. As more things were invented from the storehouse of the forest, the barn became more distinctive. The settler rose from the squalor of his temporary bark hut with the dignity of a gentleman adventurer and, with only utility as inspiration, his house and his barn—but particularly the barn—became something American.

In this day it is difficult for us to realize that the early barn-builder was a farmer who, as woodsman, could cut seasoned lumber from standing trees, and with tools forged by himself, build houses of true delicate architectural merit. A man rugged in build, firm of purpose, versatile, resourceful, and often a true scholar—who could quote from the Bible or from Greek classics—such, as often as not, was our early builder of barns and bridges.

If a farmer thought himself an inexperienced carpenter during the 1700's, he might send to Philadelphia for William Pain's *Carpenter's Pocket Manual With Compleat Directions for Building a Barn*. He would find this written in fine English and prefaced with these words: "Strength and convenience are the two most essential requisites in building; the due proportion and correspondence of parts constituting a beauty that always first attracts the eye; and where that beauty is wanting, carving and decoration only excite disgust. In like manner, the affectation of gaudy dress in a man who has the misfortune to be deformed, answers to no other purpose than to invite ridicule." This suggests that the dignity of pioneer building was recognized and encouraged by the architects of that day. That a plain carpenter's manual should contain such beautifully worded wisdom is typical of early America.

The early American colonist settled in three widely separated areas. There were the Virginia colonists who came to Jamestown in 1607, the New England colonists who came to Plymouth in 1620, and the Pennsylvania Dutch who came to Philadelphia in 1683. The countryside where each pioneer settled was different, therefore the building materials used were also different, always according to what the landscape had to offer. The house of each farmer was also different, built to resemble that which he knew from over the sea. Yet all their barns had something in common and all looked as though they might have been designed by the same architect!

It might be said that the early barn is the best example of American colonial architecture. Each old barn was born of American soil and fitted to an American landscape for specific American needs. The early American home was varied in planning but generally European in design. While the Germans were building in Pennsylvania, the Dutch were farming in New York, the English were making white villages in Massachusetts and Virginia, the French were building cabins in the Maine woods. Swedes moved into Delaware and small bands of Poles, Italians, Slovaks, Finns, and Danes completed the picture of early American farmers. The barns in Europe were small, just big enough to house a few horses or cattle, but when they built an American barn, it became the symbol of a new life. From the beginning the American barn was big, like the hopes and plans for life in the New World. It was unlike anything built anywhere else. It was entirely American.

Old barns have a nostalgic attraction to American men, and although they are fast disappearing there are many who seek them out, even groups organized for their preservation. Not always knowing exactly why, we enjoy looking at hand-hewn beams with cuts as sharp as if they were done yesterday. Like looking at a family album, it gives a sense of continuity with the past. There are historic houses, mostly European in style, made into shrines for the patriotic American to see; certainly some of the early barns, which are so thoroughly American, should be made into shrines too.

We may be surprised to see articles in our newspapers about barns of the outlying countryside, and wonder why decaying and useless old buildings should command public interest. But one by one the old barn

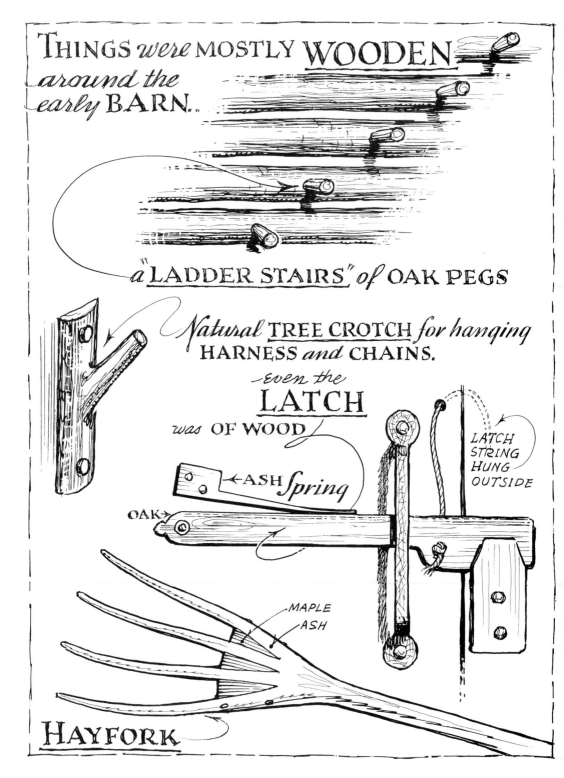

THINGS *were* MOSTLY WOODEN
around the
early BARN..

a "LADDER STAIRS" *of* OAK PEGS

Natural TREE CROTCH *for hanging*
HARNESS *and* CHAINS.

even the
LATCH
was OF WOOD

←ASH *Spring*

OAK→

LATCH
STRING
HUNG
OUTSIDE

MAPLE
ASH

HAYFORK

"collectors" are seeking out these remaining forgotten structures. Photographers find the old wood and the severe lines good for composition. Art classes gather around them with easels. Historians have found a new field. Even the family looks forward to a drive in the country with a weather eye out for old barns.

The barn is more easily spotted and is at its best during the winter months, when its severe mass complements the curves of snow-covered fields. If summer is the season of color and motion, winter is the time of stillness and form. Sun-drawn and bleached, the gray barn timbers become part of the winter landscape. The form of a barn assumes more comfortable irregularities as it settles a little each year on its weathered foundations. Whether you like it for its structural beauty or have just enough of the poet in you to see it as a symbol of pioneer man, an old farm building is the past as well as the present; vanished generations have built themselves into it. It may have outlived its usefulness as modern farming goes, but like an old apple tree that is too far gone to bear perfect fruit, its value as beauty and symbol remains.

The age of some old houses is uncertain but the history of a farmer's barn is a matter of business record, uncluttered by sentimental recollections. The date painted at the peak of a barn roof may be just an attractive touch to the antique lover, but it was put there in the same manner that a business house adds "established 1800" after its title. Barn records were kept in ledgers while the history of the old house is usually hearsay, full of romantic uncertainty. Whereas a house went up slowly, barns were usually laid out on the ground and raised with great ceremony in a day or two: the date of a barn raising was long remembered and duly recorded. There are two ancient barns near Setauket, Long Island, which the owner refers to as the "old barn" and the "new barn." The "new barn" was built in 1841 and the "old barn" was built only two years before, in 1839. It is interesting to note that although farmhouses changed with the trend of fashion from 1650 to 1850, the barn design varied little, sometimes not at all. It is as if the barn design were a standard symbol for the American Farmer: even when Victorian embellishments crept over the face of the farmer's house during the late 1850's and cluttered it with white scrollwork, the barn stubbornly remained outwardly stark, hand-hewn within.

Architecturally speaking, the pioneer builder showed his ignorance gracefully. His implements were a square, a compass, a straight-edge, and little else but good sound logic. What resulted was a severe and simple beauty without embellishment. The dynamic symmetry of barn shapes was no accident; it resulted from planning of the simplest sort, usually starting with a square or a series of squares. The sugar house shown in the drawing is from an old "standard" barn design. Lines drawn outward from a square map out two hip roofs in complete harmony with the center section and even place the door in correct composition. Designs like this appealed to the settler's love of simplicity and the "square principle" made it a plan that was easy to copy. So this same barn design may be seen repeated in farmhouses, schoolhouses, and outbuildings. The drawing also shows a saltbox shape devised in the same manner, drawn from a square and the elements of that square. This planning scheme explains why so many very old New England barns have forty-five degree roofs, fitting harmoniously into the square pattern, and not merely to carry off the heavy snowfall as architects are quick to explain.

This method of drawing lines from one point to any other point within a square in order to obtain mathematical symmetry is not always obvious when one looks at the old barn shapes, but the harmony of line is there and the result is striking. The scheme is more obvious in the well-placed windows and doors seen in some of the old houses. Today we too often place windows with no thought of putting them in artistic relation with the whole form of the house; the result is as though the builder stood at a distance and threw windows at the house, leaving them wherever they fell. In some of the later houses it is even possible to trace stairways from the outside by the erratic placing of little staircase windows. Without knowing what they really mean, people perplex their architect with an order to design a house "with nice lines, like an oldtime barn." What they are actually referring to is the dynamic symmetry of early barn design.

The only part of the barn which was copied from the old country was its roof, but even that did not last for long. Many of the settlers were expert at roof-thatching, so it was natural that the first American barns wore a thatched roof; but the severe winters of New England quickly discouraged that. Furthermore, the danger of fire both by Indian attacks of flaming arrows or by fireplace sparks was of importance. Thomas Dudley of Salem reported to the Countess of Lincoln in England that, in 1631, "Wee have ordered that noe man shall build his chimney of woode nor cover his house with thatch." Thatched roofs remained late in Pennsylvania but those in New England were quickly replaced with clapboard and bark shingles. Bark shingles were made as large as a yard square, but their irregularity and inefficiency led to wood shingles. In about 1650, shingles were nailed fast to the bottom either with small wooden pegs or with hand-cut nails. Measuring as much as a yard long and made of cedar or cypress, they were fine weatherproofing by virtue of their soft-wood ability to breathe with atmospheric changes and to contract quickly with moisture. Even now, one might be able to see daylight in a thousand places on looking up

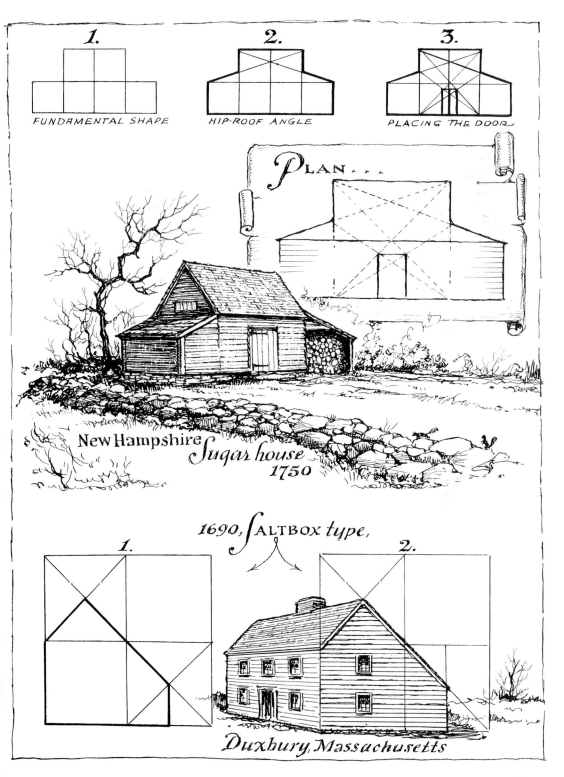

1. FUNDAMENTAL SHAPE

2. HIP·ROOF ANGLE

3. PLACING THE DOOR

PLAN...

New Hampshire *Sugar house* 1750

1690, *Saltbox type.*

1.

2.

Duxbury, Massachusetts

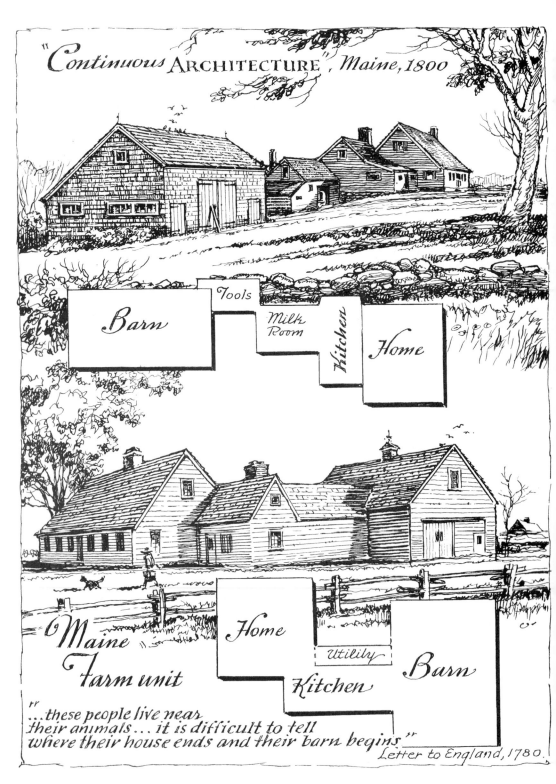

"Continuous ARCHITECTURE", Maine, 1800

Barn | Tools | Milk Room | Kitchen | Home

Maine Farm unit

Home | Utility | Kitchen | Barn

"...these people live near their animals... it is difficult to tell where their house ends and their barn begins."

Letter to England, 1780.

through the shingled roof of an old barn; yet not a drop of water will leak through, even during winter snows, because wetness draws the shingles together. Even prestorm humidity will draw shingles together. Notice also, in looking along the line of old shingle roofs, that all the nails have often come partly out, sticking up out of the smoothness of roof surface like porcupine quills. This phenomenon is caused by the years of swelling and contracting of shingles tending to "squeeze the nails out." A sped-up film of a roof during a summer shower would probably make it look as if the roof were alive and breathing.

Weather has always had a great deal to do with the planning of a barn, both for the health and comfort of the animals and for the protection of barn timbers and the stored grain. That explains why so many old barns can now be remodeled into cheerful livable houses while so few houses could be remodeled into barns. Long before the ax fell, the early barn-builder plotted out the routes of sunshine and wind, the slopes of drainage and decided just how the seasons might affect his barn site.

There seems to be no strict rule about placing the barn in reference to the farmhouse. The farmer tries to place his barn in a central manner so that in all weather the least amount of traveling is necessary. Where snows are heaviest, the idea of "continuous architecture" seems to prevail, such as seen on the early Maine farm. Here a farmer could operate his farm and take care of the animals without even leaving his roof; as one English traveler remarked in the year 1800, "The farms are like little attached villages . . . it is difficult to tell where the farmer's home ends and the stables begin."

In the Midwest where there are no hills to deflect the wind and the "snow falls horizontally," there is often a fence or even a rope stretched from the house to the barn so a farmer might not get lost on his way to the barn. This might sound ridiculous but there are many cases where a farmer missed the barn, walked in circles and finally froze to death within shouting distance of his own home. One interesting case tells of a farmer and his son, one heading toward the barn and the other leaving the barn, both with heads down struggling through a heavy snowfall. They met head-on as they turned the corner of the barn and were killed with fractured skulls. What material for a double tombstone and the quaint sort of epitaph our early tombstone carvers made!

JOHN MOODY, 1801.
Killed at noon on the fourth of November,
in raising his barn he was hit by a timber.
Be ye also ready for in such an hour
cometh the Son of Man.

Most Midwest barns are placed with their sides facing the cardinal points while many New England and Southern barns had their corners, instead, pointing to east, west, north, and south. Prevailing winds always ruled the position of buildings. Some people might insist that old barns and farmhouses were placed according to the direction of the highway without realizing that what is now a roadway was then probably only a cowpath. Old graves were usually planned so the "spirit could rise with his face to the east" but this of course was a religious practice and had nothing to do with weather.

A barn without a weathervane looks slightly naked, but, in the early days, weathervanes were used for telling wind direction and not as ornaments. The thousand and one designs of weathervanes known as Americana today are not as old as you may think. To begin with, recall that the first farmers did not believe in decoration; in fact it was part of their religion not to decorate anything—least of all, their barns. A farmer with an iron eagle or pair of spanking horses on his roof would be looked upon as showy and vulgar. The very first weathervane, believe it or not, was exactly like our aviation "windsock," a socklike piece of hanging cloth which waved in the wind. This true windsock was first used in Scotland during early golf games; it was devised to tell the velocity and direction of the wind, for at that time golf balls were called featherballs as they were filled with feathers. To play the game one had to be something of a meteorologist or have the ball carried away by the wind.

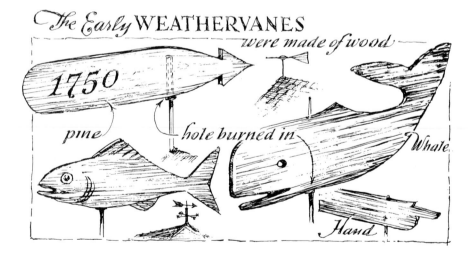

The Early WEATHERVANES were made of wood

1750 — pine — hole burned in — Whale — Hand

An early New England weathervane-maker was asked if he could design something to tell the velocity of the wind too. "What I use around these parts," said he, "is a length of chain. When the chain stands out straight, I know there's a gale a'blowin'." The joke became standard, and many of the early Yankee weathervanes contained chain motifs in them.

The early farmer kept weather records in his diary. He regarded his weather almanac highly and watched the skies frequently because his every move was either helped or hindered by weather. The weathervane on the barn was a more important instrument than a clock is on the farm today. The first weathervanes were light and sensitive, made of wood and were nothing but a simple arrow, a pointing hand, or where the barn was near the coast, a fish or whale. Most of the later weathervanes were so ponderous that only the strongest wind could move their weight. During the nineteenth century, encouraged by the Pennsylvania farmer's love of color and his ability to make things of iron, the ornate weathervane became a vogue, leading to such fancies as vanes where the wind made tiny men saw wood, ducks flap their wings, and farmers swing a scythe. But they became so complicated that few told accurately where the wind was coming from.

Living so close to nature, it is easy to understand why the settlers were weatherwise people. Today we speak of a house "nestling into a hill" or being "well located in a plot"; they spoke of a house or barn being placed "well into the weather." We speak of wood as being "weather-beaten," but they referred to it respectfully as being "weather-*cured*." Whereas we hide from weather, architecturally speaking, they were the first to utilize the movement of wind and weather. Records of early New England seem to describe colder weather than we have today; only a hundred years ago there were regular stagecoach routes over frozen lakes and rivers that now have not seen ice for years. There was a winter sled service from Staten Island to Manhattan in New York, and the Hudson River, as Currier and Ives will testify, was the rendezvous for ice-boating clubs. Water in the christening bowls of early Boston meeting houses was kept from freezing with hot coals and everyone brought his own foot-warmer. The standard New England place for keeping inks and other watery liquids was in the warm fireplace closet.

The settlers had a perfect right to be impressed with such coldness and they were quick to borrow devices from the Indians for keeping warm. One trick, that of using the insulating quality of snow as a "warming blanket" is still used in the back country of the west. On an old saltbox barn, the long slant of its roof will be facing the north or whatever direction the prevailing winter wind might be in that area. The lowest edge of the early saltbox barns reached to within a foot or two of the ground. When winter approached, it was the custom to bank this space with leaves, hay, or cornstalks mixed with sod, so that the snow could pile up over the roof from there and the wind would not reach the interior of the barn. "Slope your barn 'gainst northern blast," reads an old almanac, "and heat of day is made to last."

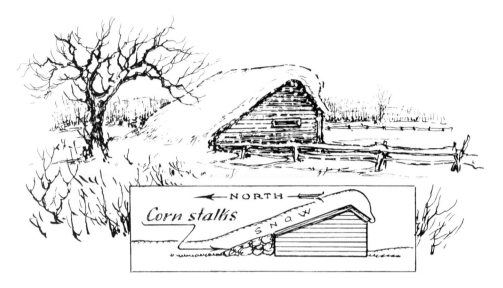

The simple gable was probably the first barn roof design, but the saltbox came quickly afterward. Many of the so-called saltboxes are really "lean-tos" because they were originally a simple gable with a later addition that makes one roof side longer than the other. The true saltbox was built around the great slant or "north roof" as it was often called. "Hips" are also found frequently to be later-year additions and "bevelly jogs" almost always were afterthoughts. "Gambrel" and "Snug Dutch" roofs were more complicated designs typical of the later 1700's; they were built by experienced builders who planned for no afterthoughts and seldom can there be seen an addition to either of these two designs.

Before the 1700's the barn, generally speaking, had no glass windows. There were merely wooden doors that swung open for light and air, or slatted louvers that were left open permanently. Sometimes there was a row of bottles "clayed" into a window recess for light to come through, but these were always changed over to glass when glass became available in America. This sounds crude to us now, but remember that the early castles of the European rich had no glass windows either, but just open slits called "wind eyes" from which the word window is derived. The louvered openings near the barn roof peaks were still called "wind eyes" before 1700. These openings are typical American devices which allow air circulation to reach the underside of the roof for preventing rot; they also keep the loft cooler during summer.

Many of the old barns were ventilated by pigeon holes, which were scattered decoratively about the upper reaches of the sidewalls. Although we now think of pigeons as being city birds, many of the early farmers preferred to keep pigeons rather than chickens. When he wanted a heavier bird for eating, he'd choose a duck or a wild turkey; but the children were given pigeon as a regular diet and pigeon pie was for the whole family. In those times wild pigeons were plentiful, often blackening the sky when they flocked. The Indians killed pigeons just for their fat and kept huge barrels of it for community use. By soaking dried reeds in melted pigeon fat, "rush lights" were made and stored as we keep matches on hand. It is strange that birds which we now regard as a great delicacy were once killed solely for their fat.

Today when we build a roof, one of the first pieces put into place is the ridge pole or ridge rafter, which is the topmost line of the roof gable. The early barn and house did not usually have this "necessary" piece of wood; it simply crossed the rafter tips and was trunneled with a mortise joint. Later (and simply in order to hold the peaked rafters in place while the rest of the roof was being worked on) a very thin board was introduced between the rafters called a ridge piece. As years went on, the barn ridge piece became more important and larger in size so that the age of later barns can often be told by the presence of this ridge piece and the size of it.

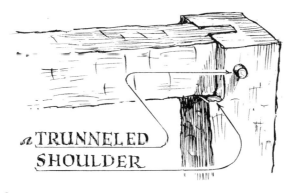

a TRUNNELED SHOULDER

When the barn roof did not have a steep pitch to spill snow off, the supporting struts within the loft had to be all the stronger. The two standard arrangements for supporting the long roof were the "post-and-collar" and the "great-strut." It was usually in the center of the middle collar that the date of the barn's raising was inscribed.

Often an aged pine is left standing close to a barn, and knowing how farmers cut trees away from their shingle roofs to avoid damp-rot, one

These were the BARN ROOFS...

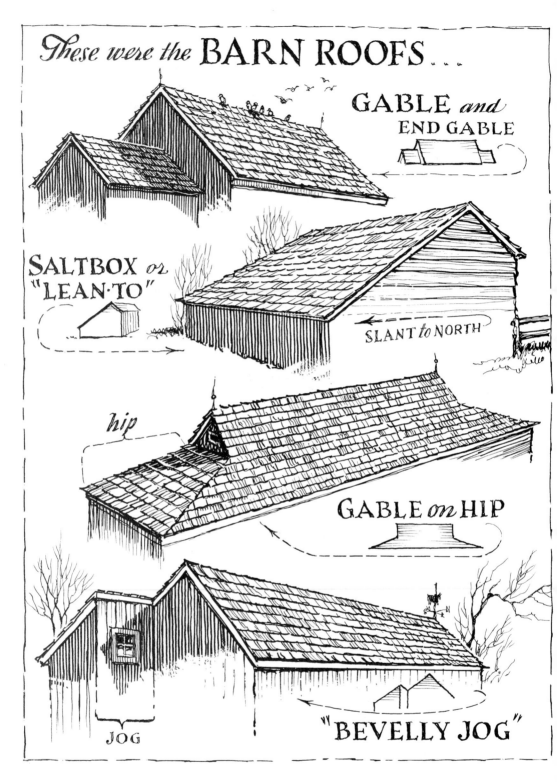

GABLE *and* END GABLE

SALTBOX *or* "LEAN-TO"

SLANT *to* NORTH

hip

GABLE *on* HIP

JOG

"BEVELLY JOG"

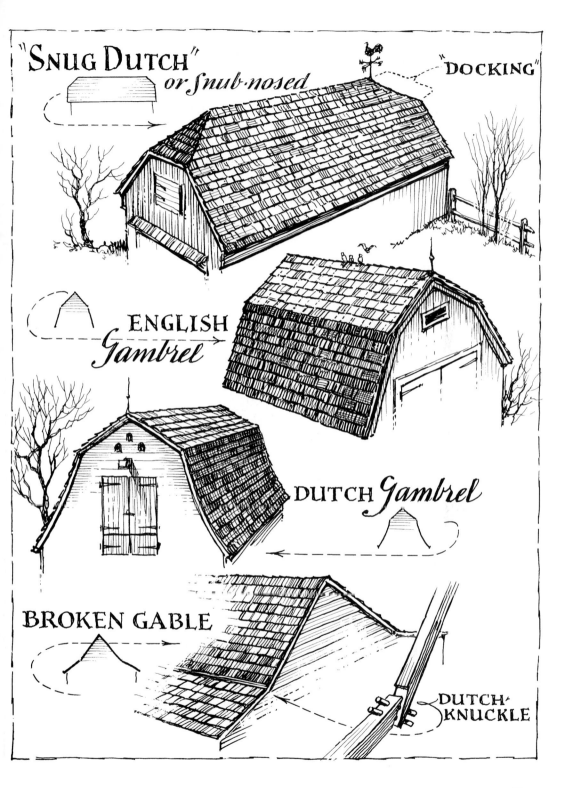

"SNUG DUTCH" or snub-nosed

"DOCKING"

ENGLISH Gambrel

DUTCH Gambrel

BROKEN GABLE

DUTCH-KNUCKLE

might wonder why. But the old-timer knew that a pine will shower its needles on roofs of its own kind with no harm. An insulating matting of moss and pine needles was valued by many and the name given to it was "pine-moss roof." There was an early saying that shingles laid in the dark of the moon would never warm, and there are still "shinglin' nights" among the mountain folk of the South. Whether it is superstition or science is problematical, but some of the old pine-moss roofs laid in the dark of the moon are still flat and waterproof after a hundred years of weather.

Modern shingles are dipped in a preservative, but the oldest shingles were placed on raw. There are mentions of soaking, heating, and even smearing shingles with cow dung, but generally speaking the change from bark covering to shingle covering involved no preservative measures. The right wood in the right place will need no paint. The locust posts that have outlived several sets of wire, the ancient cypress sewer pipes of New York, and the shingles that are still serviceable although the holes still show where their nails have long since disintegrated, vouch for the soundness of wood. Not until the end of the eighteenth century did it seem necessary to paint wood. Even the earliest bridges went unpainted despite the continual splashing of water and the general dampness of river sites. Moss-covered and green with age, the remaining bridge timbers seem to have rotted only as much as iron would have rusted.

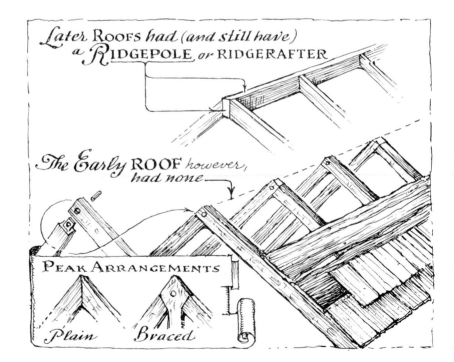

In the earliest settlements it would have been considered a useless extravagance to paint one's house and to paint the barn would be vulgar and showy. But toward the end of the eighteenth century the art of wood seasoning gave way to the art of artificial preservation and the farmer became paint-conscious. Ready-made paint was entirely unavailable and so, like everything else, it had to be made at the farm. The Virginia settlements began painting first and their paints had the quality of stains sinking into the wood as much as covering it over. Using lampblack consistently, they evolved a fine taste for grayish pastel shades. For outbuildings, the color red vied with ocher or "oaker" as the word was often spelled. Such announcements were seen as, "To be sold, two dwelling houses, kitchen, storehouse, dairy, and meat house, all painted in ochre [October 17, 1776]."

The northern farmer had not the Virginian's accessibility to the colors and oils; if he were to paint, he wanted something he could raise on the farm as well as mix at home. He found that red oxide of iron and skim milk with lime added made a plastic-like coating that hardened quickly and lasted for many years, giving birth to our famous American "barn red." The theory that barn red was taken from the Indians and that blood was used, though not true, is not without some foundation. As an idea taken from the Indians, farm-stock blood was used in the very beginning, mixed with milk and used for decorating cupboards and interior surfaces. But

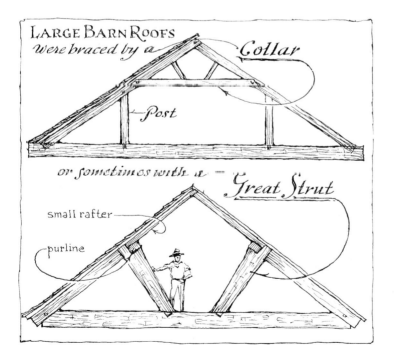

LARGE BARN ROOFS were braced by a Collar

Post

or sometimes with a Great Strut

small rafter

purline

limited quantities of blood and its lack of preserving qualities made the mixture useless for large surfaces and, of course, for outside painting. Another red that was taken from Indian lore, called both turkey red and Indian red, was made from clay mixed with the whites of wild turkey eggs. Turkey blood added to the mixture gave it a deeper mahogany shade.

Even as late as 1850, milk was being used to make paint. Here is a recipe taken from an 1835 Almanac:

TO MAKE FARM PAINT

skimmed milk	4 lbs. or half gallon
lime	6 ounces
linseed oil or neatsfoot (cow's hoof glue)	4 ounces
color	1 and a half pounds.

(for outside painting, add 2 ounces of slacked lime, oil, and turpentine.)

The milk-base paint hardened so well that it often caked off in sheets where it had failed to soak into soft wood. Linseed oil was found to have that needed soaking quality and when it was introduced as a paint base, a new farm crop appeared. Farmers pressed oil from their own flaxseed and soon no barn or toolshed was without a few barrels of the stuff. Red was now accepted as a standard color for the barn; the color was found to be warmer in winter because it absorbed the sun's rays. The red oxide was available and the mixture became six pounds of Venetian red (35 percent sesquioxide of iron ground in oil) with one pound of rosin and thinned with four gallons of raw linseed oil.

Thus the traditional red of the barn is the result of function rather than of decoration or even, as some writings have hinted, superstition. Because it was considered unnecessary to paint the "right wood in the right place," many of the old-timers sneered at their neighbors' newly painted barn and accused them of copying the "superstitious Germans of Pennsylvania." Actually copying from these German and Dutch barns was just an expression of color starvation from the somber New England colorings.

Red clay was plentiful in Pennsylvania and the European sense of color ran riot with red bricks, red cows, red geraniums, and red barns. Of course, when the Pennsylvania Dutch farmer added a big ornamental design and, for lack of a better explanation, said it was "just for luck," he was accused of having designed a hex sign to frighten away the devil. Actually these so-called hex signs have no more superstition in them than the same designs that appear in any farmwife's quilt. The designs for a patchwork quilt were made with a ruler and a compass; the farmer borrowed the same idea for his hex sign. To guard against lightning or fire or disease to the cattle? With tongue in cheek, perhaps yes, but in the same manner as we today pick up a four-leaf clover or hang a horseshoe over a door. At one time the farmer wore a red stocking or a piece of red in his hat for the same reason that a hunter wears a bright red hat—to distinguish him from game and to protect him from hunters. It was the custom for a farmwife to send her husband off to the fields with a red handkerchief or flag of some sort for him to wear or to hang nearby so that she could see him from a distance. From all this evolved the farmer's red bandanna which he wore around his neck as much for identification as for soaking up the sweat. For awhile the southern farmer accused the northern farmer of wearing the red bandanna for superstitious reasons, but today, of course, we never even hear of such nonsense.

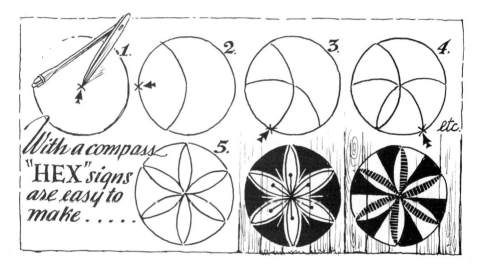

Superstition had very little place on the early farmstead. Some of the European folklore reached our countryside, but the farming man's sense of humor always laughed down banshees, fairies, and luck charms. Our folklore began in a printing age so that the characters in them could not be illogical nor could the tales get taller with each repeating as with word-of-mouth folklore. Dull as it sounds, our folklore is mostly built up around real people like Casey Jones, John Henry, Johnny Appleseed, and Davey Crockett. Duller still in comparison with ogres and witches, our folklore sounds a note of mission and a sense of responsibility.

When England imposed a large tax on metal, the settlers saved every piece of scrap iron they could get their hands on. If a horse threw a shoe it was as bad luck as if you had lost one of your own shoes, and finding it was, naturally, lucky. Yet the idea has grown up that anyone who now finds a horseshoe automatically acquires luck. Carpenters in the old days always tapped a finished piece of timber with their knuckles with a "well, that's that" attitude. From that small gesture Americans have coined a phrase and when they are through work and ready to go home they are said to "knock off." "Knocking on wood" also was revived in a similar way. Originally a Druid gesture of worship, knocking on wood at the barn door was a farming habit many years ago. When the stock had been taken care of and the team bedded down for the night, the farmer closed the barn with, we might imagine, a silent prayer that no harm would befall it. After closing the door, it was the habit to touch the wood of the doorframe with a rap for luck, and we have ever since been knocking on wood when we hope for the best.

Early American farm life has influenced many of our present-day customs. No one was more aware of the connection that the barn has with

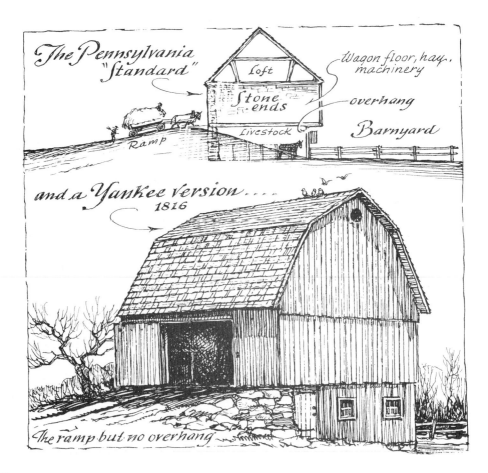

The Pennsylvania "Standard"

Loft

Wagon floor, hay, machinery

Stone ends

overhang

Ramp

Livestock

Barnyard

and a Yankee version....
1816

The ramp but no overhang

Christmas than the farmer. Christ, of course, was born in a barn. The children were told that on Christmas night the cattle spoke and kneeled in honor of the Saviour. Gifts were left in the barn for the children to find in the morning, and to keep them away from the barn while the presents were being prepared, the legend was that misfortune would befall anyone who listened to the cattle "speak" on Christmas Eve. Although we hang a Christmas wreath on the door of our house now, it was once hung on the barn door, and the cattle were dressed in garlands and fancy ribbons for Christmas day. All this, however, occurred after 1740 for up until that time Christmas was just another working day in America, particularly for the Puritan who had strict laws against any kind of Christmas celebration. In 1740, the Moravians founded Bethlehem in Pennsylvania and began the Christmas as we now know it, done up in a German manner with Saint Nicholas and all.

Hallowe'en was originally the eve of All Saints' Day, and it became confused with All Souls' Day which is the time that the living pray for the souls of the dead. But the unorthodox way that we now celebrate the "eve of All Saints' Day" with witches, the farm broom, pumpkins, apples, and cornstalks, leaves little doubt but that it all originated on the farm.

The very first barns were experiments. Without architectural merit, they were the temporary shelters that were thrown up when winter came, and were like the caves and mud shelters that the settlers themselves lived in before they had the time to erect a suitable house. Except to bring home the misery of those first months, there is little reason to discuss the construction of the first barns. What we are most concerned with are the barns beginning with the eighteenth century for with seventy-five years of New World agriculture behind them, the settler had really turned farmer and had evolved a rural American culture that was reflected in the things he built. Certain touches in design became typical of the countryside and one could soon pick out the Pennsylvania barn by its stonework and the way it nestled into a hill, the Maine barn by the way it was attached to the farmhouse, and the Western barn by its high peak and great roof sweep to the northwest.

The credit for a standard early American barn design stands between two camps—that of New England and that of Pennsylvania. Pennsylvania barns contain several "first" factors and they have indeed been copied, but they are too distinctive to be a standard or average. The barns of Pennsylvania used stone and red brick; they specialized in an overhang which they called an "overshoot," or an overshot loft. Their mixed architectural design often sported decorations. Such features as these are not at all standard in other early barns, but the following *have* been borrowed throughout the country. The Pennsylvania barn was usually placed against a hill. It most often faced south and had a number of Dutch doors opening into the barnyard, its north side snuggled into the protection of the hill. Its second floor was usually accessible from the hilltop, and when there was no hill, a dirt ramp was constructed. In this manner, harvests could be taken directly to the loft and stored without hoisting. The ground floor housed the livestock and with one end of the barn snuggling into the warmth of the hill, the other end faced south where Dutch doors opened into the barnyard. This arrangement was a good one and replicas of it crossed the Alleghenies with very few changes. Both Yankee and Southerner copied the general lay-out, but the other Swiss and German features stayed right in Pennsylvania.

The Mennonites of 1700 built for permanency; they had little faith in any wood but oak and they used stone wherever possible. Asked why he'd built a barn wall five feet wide, a Mennonite gave the classic reply, "Why not?" Whereas most of the early barns of New England are gasping their last at the present time, many of the stone Pennsylvania barns are good for another two hundred years, even though they are agriculturally outmoded. The Western copies of the Pennsylvania barn seem only to have grasped the interior arrangement and the habit for making everything big. The fine carpentering became scarce, the wood seasoning was poor and bark was left on some of the timbers. But there was less attempt at permanency during the agricultural trek toward the West.

There is no record of any "first" Western barn. The farmer who first moved into the promising West must have been a perplexed person, for everything was vastly different. Wood was scarce on the plains, water could not be depended upon, and all the methods of preparing for winter that the farmer had learned in the East were useless on the flat stretches of open land. The first Western barns were cattle shelters made of nothing but poles and straw. A middle-nineteenth century book, *Barn Plans and Outbuildings*, says: "Farmers in the newer portions of the west do not have stables for their cattle or snug sheds for their sheep. Stock raisers are called upon to make the winter as comfortable as possible for their animals with the limited means at their command. Sheds of poles with roofs of straw are extensively used and with profit . . . they furnish at the same time, shelter from storms and feed for the protected animals. New hay is packed on after each storm. Those who have traveled over the cattle ranges of the west have been struck with the skill displayed in the construction of these shelters. The only trouble with them is that they are so satisfactory that the farmers are apt to forget that they are temporary and build nothing to replace them."

70

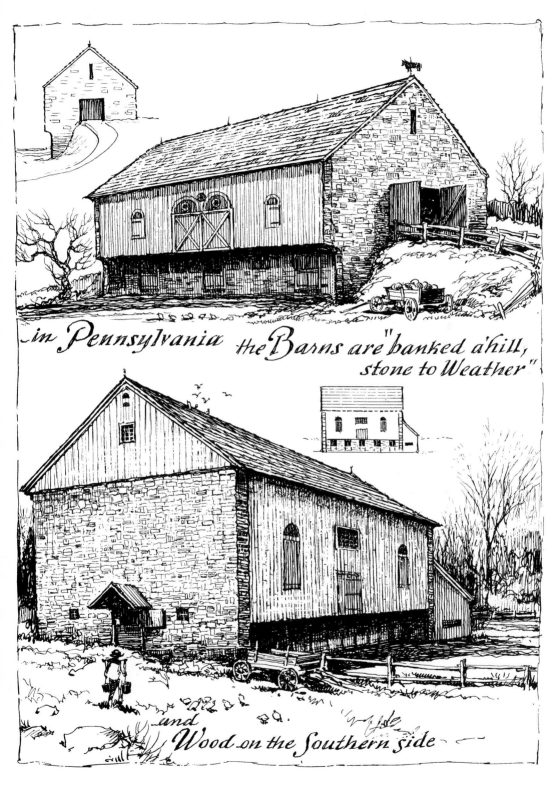

in Pennsylvania the "Barns are "banked a'hill, stone to Weather"

and Wood on the Southern side

71

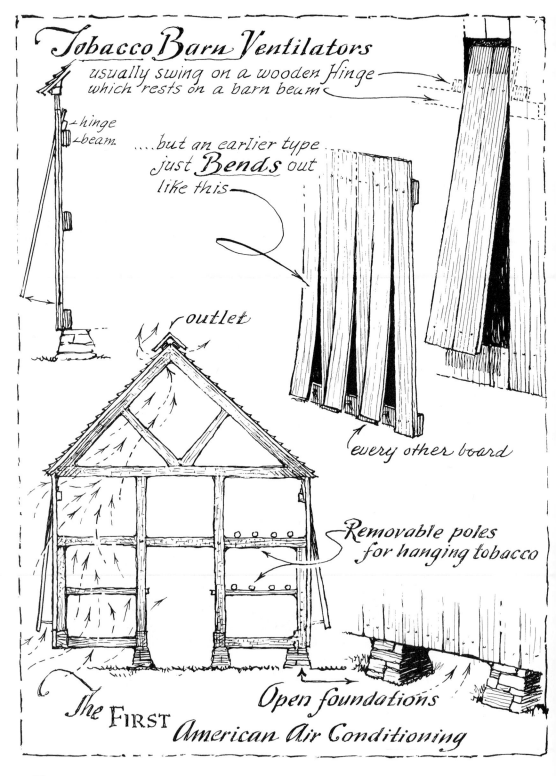

Tobacco Barn Ventilators

usually swing on a wooden Hinge
which rests on a barn beam

hinge
beam.

...but an earlier type
just **Bends** out
like this

outlet

every other board

Removable poles
for hanging tobacco

Open foundations

The FIRST American Air Conditioning

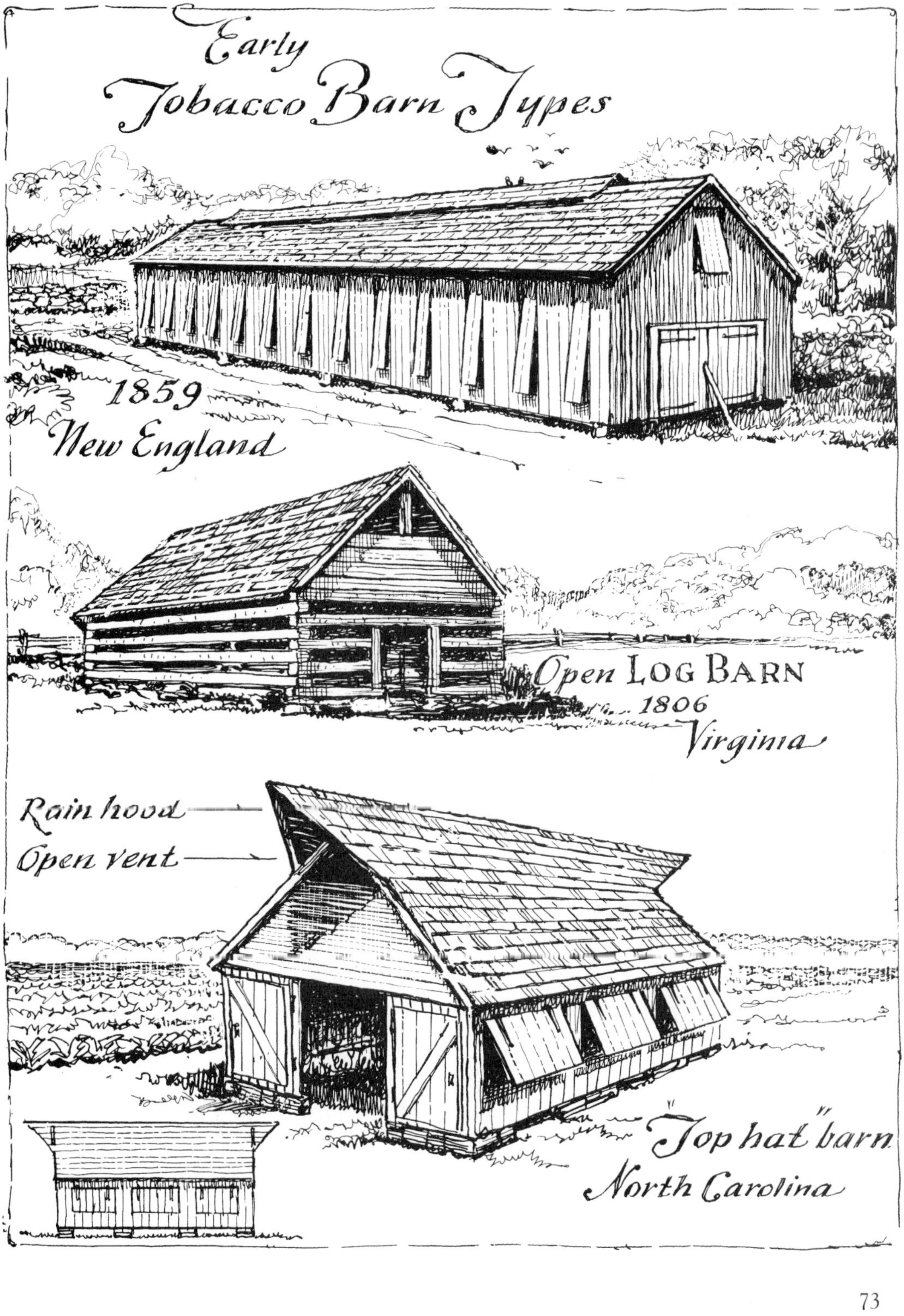

Early
Tobacco Barn Types

1859
New England

Open LOG BARN
1806
Virginia

Rain hood
Open vent

"Top hat" barn
North Carolina

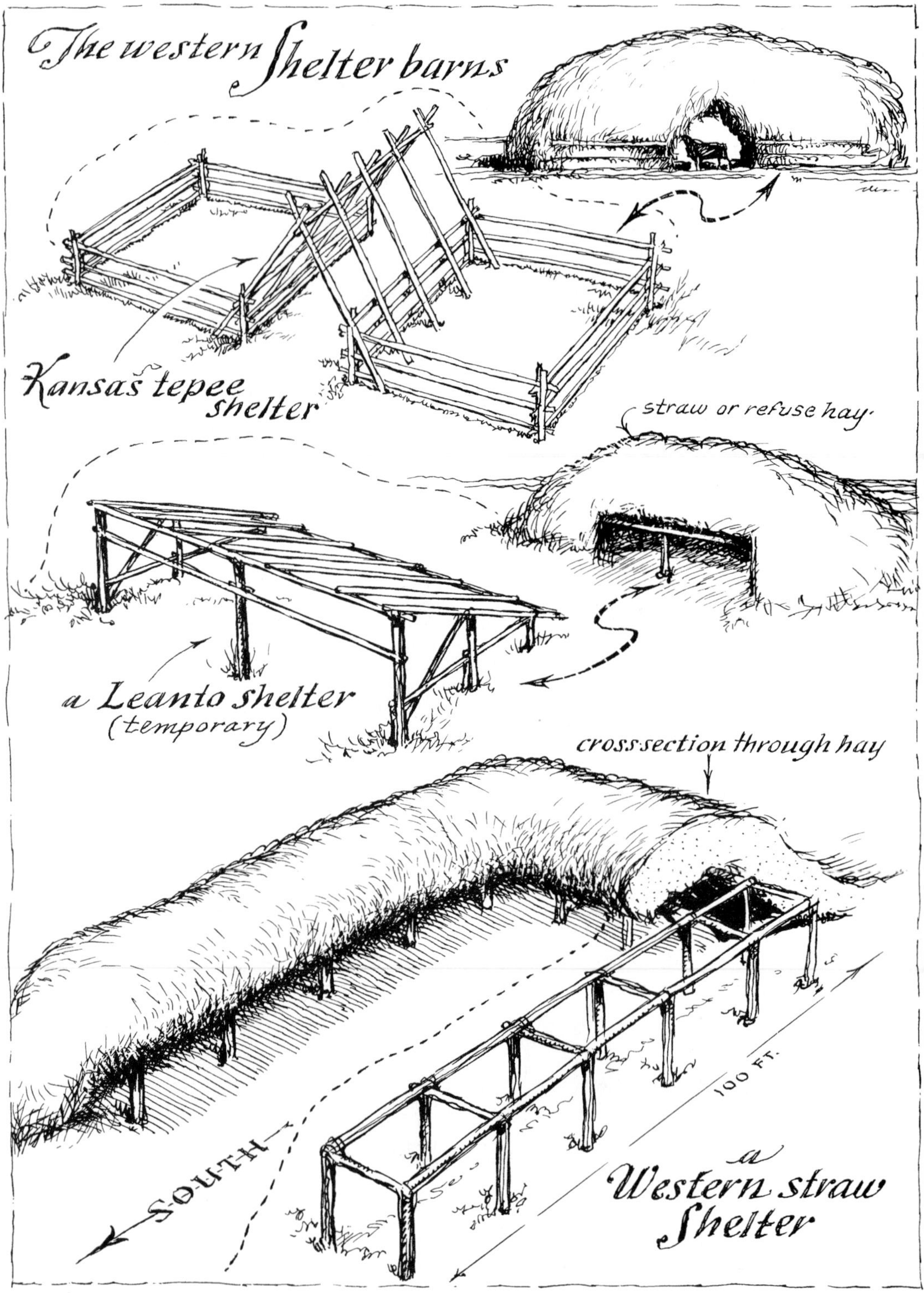

The western Shelter barns

Kansas tepee shelter

a Leanto shelter
(temporary)

straw or refuse hay.

cross section through hay

SOUTH

100 FT.

a
Western straw
Shelter

The field shelter of the West was really an adoption of the haystack or "field barn" as the built-up haystack was called. Farmers now call them "stack silos." The early farms had beautifully built stacks, often covered with conical shingled roofs that were raised for new hay to be added. A 1954 copy of *Farm Quarterly* reads: "Do we need any barns for beef cattle? The field barn that is built right where the hay is cut, and cattle feed through stanchions below it, makes an ideal wind shelter and automatic feeding station." Which shows that some of the old ideas of farming might still return.

Although we think of a silo as being something tall, the word "silo" is from the French and its meaning is "a pit." The trench silo has been with us longer than the stack idea; either on the surface or in a trench, the silage was packed in a pile running north and south. With no cover at all except ground limestone and sawdust, a correctly packed stack silo will have

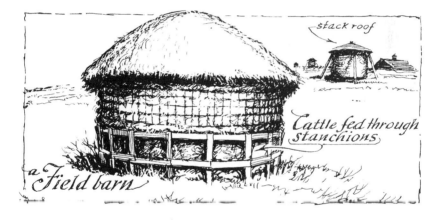

a Field barn
stack roof
Cattle fed through stanchions

no more spoilage than a few inches on top and about a foot on either side. They can be built right where the grass is cut, which saves labor for the farmer; for this reason you seldom saw an upright wooden silo on the earliest farms. Besides, there were not a great number of milch cows to be fed. Cows in those days were most important for use in breeding the oxen which were the tractors of their day.

The great dryness of the flat country made many of the rules of barn-building learned in the East useless. Trunnels came loose in the high-altitude air, and mortise joints creaked in the western winds. By the time that barns were being built in the West, iron bolts and screws were already being made, so the old wooden trunnels were not always used. One way of making wood trunnels· hold better was a western custom of "nicking" the trunnel before hammering it in. This idea came from the habit of doing

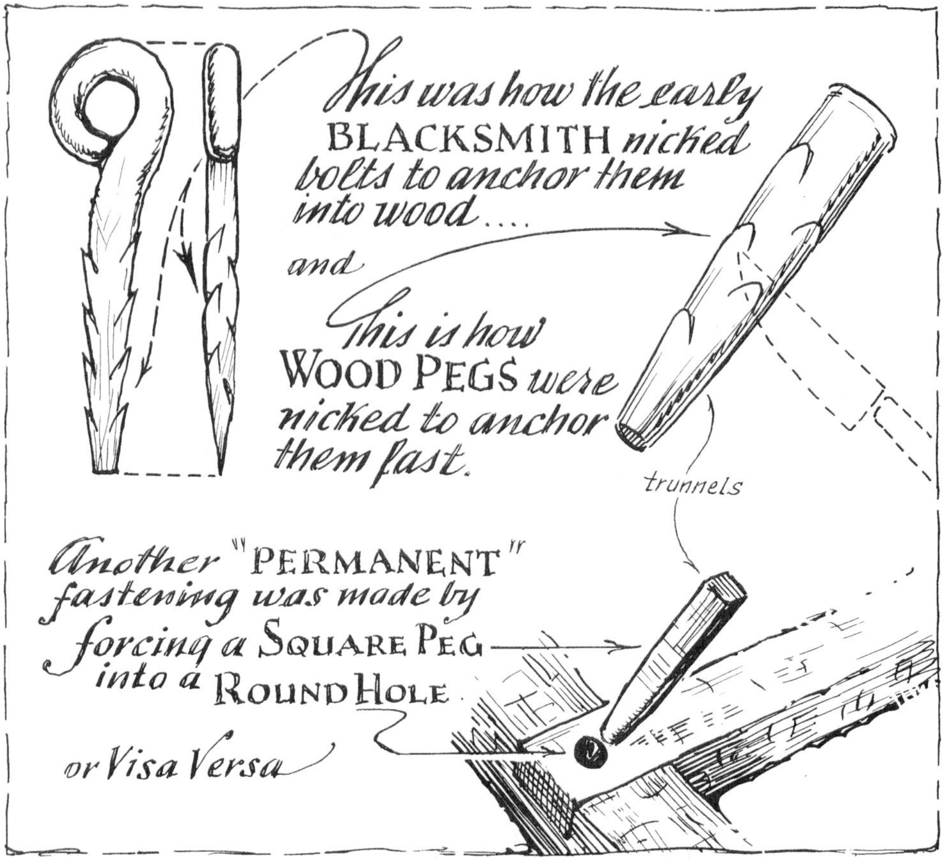

This was how the early BLACKSMITH *nicked bolts to anchor them into wood....*

and

This is how WOOD PEGS *were nicked to anchor them fast.*

trunnels

Another "PERMANENT" *fastening was made by forcing a* SQUARE PEG *into a* ROUND HOLE

or Visa Versa

the same thing to iron gate-post bolts to keep them from coming loose, as the drawing shows.

The barns of the West were not without the dignity and romance of American farm life, but the change from eastern farming was such that many of the arts of woodworking and seasoning were lost in the transition. But even changes and mistakes are sometimes healthy. In 1844, the Wales bull Chance broke out of his pen and on February 13, 1845, "Sir David 68 was born," who turned out to be the greatest show bull of all time. As one Hereford breeder said, "Thank God for those poorly seasoned and brittle boards."

What the barn lost by way of carpentry in its trip westward, it made up for in simplicity and size. As delightful as the eastern barn is by being a part of the landscape, the western barn is impressive by breaking away from the flatness. Sudden, massive, like a ship at sea, the western barn is distinctive. The flat country became a proving ground for many new ideas in barn-building. In the middle of the nineteenth century, the rich farmers of the East were inspired by the American's gift for invention;

the West was new so why not move westward, go whole hog, and try one's hand at new barn designing? One of the more radical ideas to come out of that age was the round barn which is still being tried out today. The famed octagon house of 1850 was preceded by the octagon and circular barn of 1830. Designed at a time when the farmer had risen his fastest in the national scene, many things were being done to modernize the farm and make farming easier. Planned on the theory that a circle encloses the maximum amount of floorspace with a minimum of wall, the idea was good but the proof was poor. Hay storage required complicated devices for loading, and the pie-shaped stalls would have been best only for pie-shaped animals. The expense of building these round-shaped barns and the risk of endangering the whole structure by one weak bit of engineering made of the round barns experiments that failed. The idea caught on, however, as a new way of building houses and around 1848, Orson S. Fowler presented the octagon house as a solution for all those who wanted to get away from the conventional rectangular form. It made a better house than it did a barn

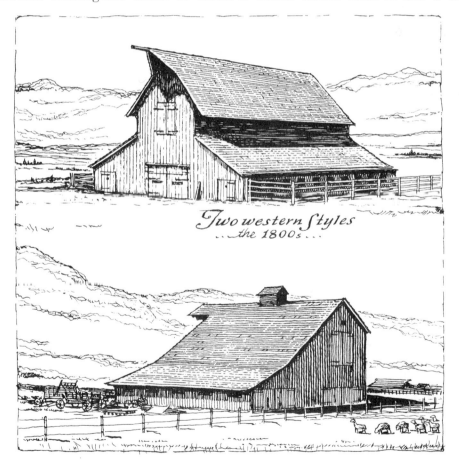

Two western Styles
...the 1800s...

because it gave more window space for each room and it provided a thousand pie-shaped closets and spaces for water tanks and gadgets. It lasted longer than the octagon barn, but only a few octagon houses were built and those still standing are looked upon as no more than American curiosities.

When the farmer builds his house he draws a rough sketch for the architect, but when he builds his barn you will find him sitting up nights planning and expressing himself in design. He knows that the welfare of his family depends upon the comfort of his cattle. No matter how things change on the farm, the biggest and most expensive thing there will always be the barn.

To the farmer of today, the early barn has become as useless as a pair of oxen or a kerosene lamp. The farm has become so changed that within the next few years not one of the old architectural features will have remained. But as long as man farms, which is as long as the world eats, there will still be the smell of hay and the sounds of farm life and with them a great respect for the farmer of the past who was poor equipment-wise but so rich in having lived the American life to its fullest. Ruskin said that one cannot love art better than to love what it reflects; while there are still farmers who find sentimental attraction in the early barns, you may be sure that the typical farmer still lives. And as long as there is an urge to preserve the personality of the people who created these things, the typical American still lives.

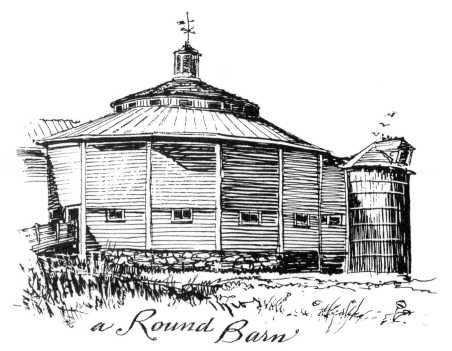

a Round Barn

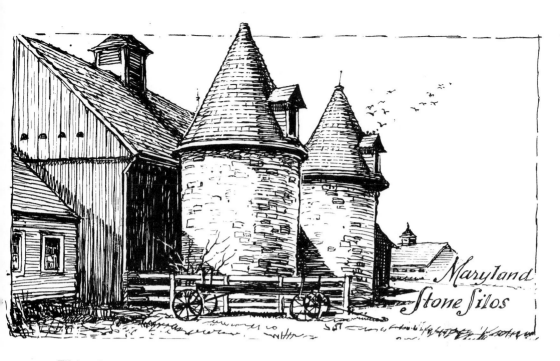

Maryland
Stone Silos

This chapter ends here, but in a more important way it will continue, because the reader will now notice many of the old barns where before he might have looked without seeing.

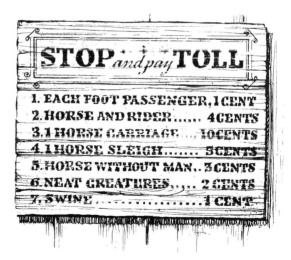

STOP *and pay* TOLL

1. EACH FOOT PASSENGER, 1 CENT
2. HORSE AND RIDER...... 4 CENTS
3. 1 HORSE CARRIAGE.... 10 CENTS
4. 1 HORSE SLEIGH........ 5 CENTS
5. HORSE WITHOUT MAN.. 3 CENTS
6. NEAT CREATURES,.,... 2 CENTS
7. SWINE .... 1 CENT

The BRIDGES

We crossed the river by a wooden bridge, roofed and covered on all sides, and nearly a mile in length. It was profoundly dark; perplexed with great beams, crossing and recrossing it at every possible angle; and through the broad chinks and crevices in the floor, the rapid river gleamed, far down below, like a legion of eyes. We had no lamps; and as the horses stumbled and floundered through this place, toward the distant speck of dying light, it seemed interminable. I really could not at first persuade myself as we rumbled heavily on, filling the bridge with hollow noises, and I held down my head to save it from the rafters above, but that I was in a painful dream; for I had often dreamed of toiling through such places, and as often argued, even at the time, "This cannot be reality."

—CHARLES DICKENS, 1842

THE COVERED BRIDGES came much later than the first barns. In fact, covered bridges are not as old as most people think. The first American bridge patent was for a covered bridge and it was issued on January 21, 1797, to Charles W. Peale, the famed painter of George Washington. He became interested in bridges as a member of the Town Board of Philadelphia. Recognized as a great artist and designer, he was called upon to plan a bridge over the Schuylkill. Eight years later, a bridge was built by Timothy Palmer on the site suggested by Peale, but Peale's bridge never got beyond his paper plans. The *Railroad Gazette* for October 8, 1886, comments: "When the Market Street Bridge was finished in 1804 it was the intention that it should remain open, free to action of the sun and air, exposed as well to rain and storm. Judge Richard Peters, a prominent stockholder of the company which erected the bridge, was the author of the plan of covering it at the sides and surmounting it with a roof. It was his opinion that if the timbers were left open and the roadway exposed to the alternate action of storms that would soon lead to decay and destruction. So the sides were boarded up, with the exception of spaces for windows. A long roof was placed over it, and the bridge was nothing more than a wooden tunnel, leading from one side of the river to the other." And so, as far as most experts agree, the American covered bridge was born.

As shown on the following page, the earliest of American bridges were "corduroy" in construction, just logs stretched across supporting timbers. Next came variations of arches and trusses, but the span was always no greater than could be negotiated with one single stick or long timber; in other words, there were always just two stringers side by side, arched or trussed for strength. In 1785, however, Enoch Hale put a bridge over the Connecticut River at Bellows Falls: it was three hundred and sixty-five feet long and it was the first American bridge with spans greater than the previous one "strengthened" stringer type. Variations of this new type called for the necessary joints to be boxed in for protection from weather. The timbers were pinned together with turned white oak dowels dipped in linseed oil and the complete trusses were boxed in with soft pine to "soak" the dampness away from the bridge itself. As shown in the drawings, the top plank or weatherplate was always slanted to take the rain away. The

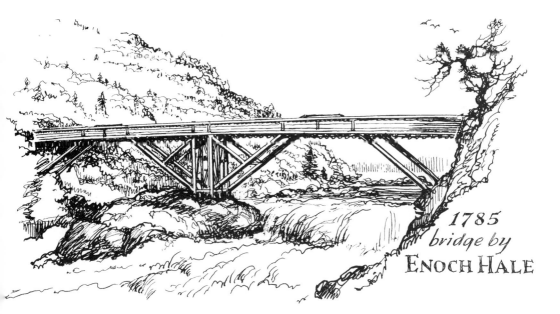

1785
bridge by
ENOCH HALE

Evolution of the Covered Bridge......

First... the CORDUROY bridge of LOGS..1650
Without bracing
1

2 a TRUSS *added,* then
BOXED *in from the* WEATHER

1700

3

1790
Open bridge
West Dover, Vt.

4 Then PARTIALLY
ROOFED
(BRIDGE OVER *the* MOHAWK *1810*)

Riverton, Connecticut, example slants its top sideways and away from the roadway while the West Dover, Vermont, example slants with the roadway in peaked roofs. It is easy to see how this boxing suggested a complete housing and an eventual covered bridge; most of these partly covered or boxed bridges were roofed over later and only the shorter spans like the West Dover and the Riverton bridges remained open. The Mohawk Bridge shown in the drawing was built in 1808, but was not covered with siding and roofing until some time between 1825 and 1830. Notice that the toll-house end is completely covered. Like many of the early bridges, it was anything but beautiful; their charm lay first in their eloquent expression as a symbol of the era in which they were built; secondly in their ability to become, as the barn did, part of the setting and rooted in the countryside. This effect gives rise to the saying that all covered bridges look alike, yet taken away from their setting, they would have appeared very different.

Disappearing at a rate of almost one a day, there are now about two thousand covered bridges, some still used, many hiding out their declining years just beyond sight of the new highway and the concrete bridge that has replaced it. And some there are that are not only hidden but forgotten as well, their ruins crumbling back into the landscape from which they came. There are covered bridges in thirty-three States, with Pennsylvania in the lead. Next comes Ohio, which surprises most people who think of the covered bridge as existing only in New England, and then, believe it or not, comes Indiana. Fourth on the list is Oregon and fifth (though most think it is first) is Vermont, so often called the "covered bridge state." Although the rate of destruction makes the count impermanent, the list probably carries on with Alabama, West Virginia, New Hampshire, Kentucky, New York, and California in that order.

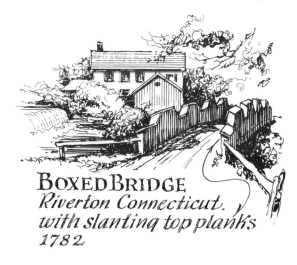

BOXED BRIDGE
Riverton Connecticut.
with slanting top planks
1782

If the old American covered bridge is passing into oblivion, the floating bridge has already gone—except for one lone example, the Floating Bridge at Brookfield, Vermont. Built in 1936 by the State and the Town of Brookfield at a joint cost of twelve thousand dollars, this structure is the fifth of its kind to be floated over Colt's Pond since 1810. Three hundred eighty oak barrels, hot-dipped in tar and chained together, keep its 320 feet of framework afloat to the joy of the townspeople who steadfastly refuse the highway department's offer of a new bridge to replace it. Perhaps they feel it is a monument to the resourcefulness of Brookfield's early settlers and perhaps they are thinking back to the legend that gave their floating bridge its birth. The pond, it seems, was too wide for a single span and its mud bottom offered no possibilities of sinking piers for multiple spans. Despite the warnings of the selectmen, many townspeople continued to take advantage of the short cut over the frozen pond during winter until one man broke through and drowned. After a meeting it was decided to stretch a raftlike path of logs, chained together, right on top of the ice so that people could walk over it with some safety in case of weak ice during a thaw. When the ice finally did melt, the raft became a bridge, floating perfectly by means of its well-seasoned logs. In this manner, although only usable in ponds and still water, the New England floating bridge was born.

Although the first pioneers never saw one, the covered bridges are just old enough to be an important link in American history; they seem to mark the difference between the day of the horse and buggy and the automobile. Just as Washington was supposed to have slept in an unending number of houses, he was also reputed to have crossed many covered bridges which were built fifty years after his death. Even today, Connecticut people are bringing out written proof that Washington crossed their famous covered Bull's Bridge. Washington did cross an open bridge near that site, but the present bridge there was built by Jacob Bull in 1858.

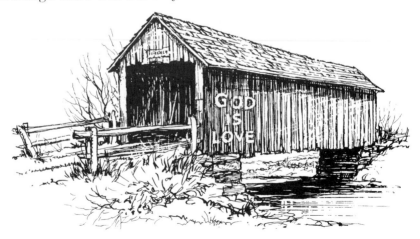

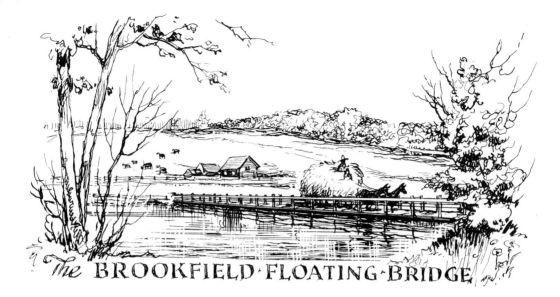

The BROOKFIELD·FLOATING·BRIDGE

The experts seem to agree that the roof of the covered bridge was merely to protect it and nearly all of their accounts mention the farmer who explained that bridges were covered for the same reason that women wear petticoats—"to protect their underpinning." This is true to a great extent—witness the fact that many of the earlier bridges had no roofs although the trusses on both sides were boxed in with, of course, narrow roofs or top boards across each protective housing. But after collecting all the various reasons that the "ancient people" have given for covering their bridges and analyzing them, it might be that there is not one reason but many. Six sound reasons are as follows:

To keep water out of the joints, where it might freeze during winter or cause rotting during summer.

To keep the roadway dry, for the inner floor was often oiled and was slippery if it became wet from rain.

To strengthen the structure; the added weight more than made up its bulk by making the bridge more solid.

To give the bridge a barn appearance; farm animals did not relish crossing a rushing river and were more liable to run and not walk.

To keep the bridge from drying out; in very hot weather, the bridge would tend to dry out and loosen, causing it to creak and sag.

To keep the snow off; although this was the commonest reason given, it does not seem the best. It is true that during a heavy snowfall, although the highway could be cleared, an open bridge would keep the snow "encased." During most snowfalls, it was necessary for the toll-keeper to "snow-pave" the interior for everyone used sleds during winter in those days.

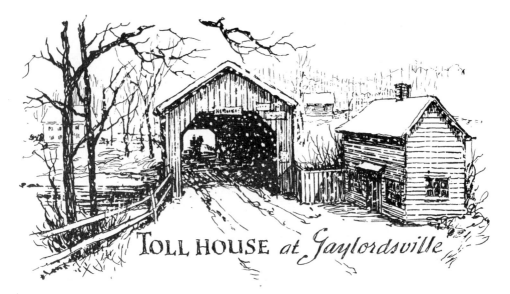

TOLL HOUSE *at Gaylordsville*

People ask why early American bridges were built of wood without remembering that almost everything a hundred years ago was made of wood. Expense had little to do with it. Although records of bridges costing a few hundred dollars will impress us today, we forget that a few hundred dollars then is equal to many thousands now. One public scandal involved eight hundred dollars for labor on the Trumansburg bridge in New York State, but a fairer price for the cost of the average covered bridge seems to be between one and three thousand dollars. In 1857, bridge carpenters were paid sixty to sixty-five cents a day, a salary which included, however, three meals.

Here is one of the earliest records of what it used to cost to build a bridge. The date was 1780, which was before the time of covered bridges so it is presumed to be for a simple open bridge.

BILL FOR BRIDGE BUILDING

114 days work chopping	22	6s
20 days work hewing	6	6
42½ days ox work	4	5
2900 feet of plank	4	7
1500 feet of boards	1	10
Pine timber	1	10

The committee met to vote on this bridge on October 20, 1780, and the bill was receipted on August 10, 1781. Not a bad record for speed particularly when the work was done through the snows of winter and the rains of spring.

Let's take a typical, average mid-century American covered bridge and thumb through some of the transaction papers to see what such a structure costs and how it was built. In 1832, little help could be expected from county, state, or town authorities, but the factories, grist mills, sawmills, and a cutlery works near Gaylordsville, Connecticut, needed a new bridge badly. Oak, chestnut, walnut, and pine grew tall in the nearby hills and the present bridge had seen its day. So a group of businessmen organized the Gaylordsville Toll Bridge Company and agreed to build a covered bridge and maintain it "for the convenience and safety of the travelling public." Shares sold for twenty-five dollars and fourteen hundred dollars was raised: eventually the bridge cost $1,500.14, including:

4000 feet of two-inch oak floor planks	$100.00
1800 feet of long string pieces	324.00
Mud sills of heavy chestnut timber	25.00
Boards to cover the bridge	60.00
Carpenter work complete	400.00

A full day's work of ten hours for a man and a pair of horses was worth two dollars and fifty cents, a man and his ox team charged two dollars. The wood came from the surrounding hills and ox teams hauled the logs to a nearby sawmill. The price of fifteen hundred dollars included leveling and grading the road approaches and hauling the stone for the abutments from a marble quarry a mile away. A bill was proposed to raise two cents on the dollar (payable in grain) for the repair of the bridge, if damage were caused by flood or freshet. The bridge was washed out completely in 1854. The second bridge was built in 1876 and the cost indicated a hundred percent increase in values, for that bridge cost three thousand dollars.

Sometimes a bridge such as the Gaylordsville bridge was named after the town it was near, but often, when buildings started being built around a secluded bridge, the community finally took on the name of the bridge. But a covered bridge seldom remained nameless. One Ohio bridge was named by children who were chased by its irritable old toll collector; it was known as Old Meaney's Bridge. Old Maid Parker Bridge in Rutland, Vermont, got its name from the caustic old maiden who owned the land on one side of the bridge. Another bridge in Indiana had fine broad sideboards that disappeared with annoying regularity. When it was found that the boards were being stolen and used for wall-papering boards, the bridge was from that time on known as Papering Board Bridge.

One bridge in southern Ohio received a coat of fine red paint by a patent medicine company for the privilege of advertising rights on its sides.

The sign which spelled out WIZARD OIL in ten foot letters had such publicity value that the bridge soon became known as the Wizard Oil Bridge. That old bridge is long gone but the modern highway bridge built recently at the same site is still called the Wizard Oil Bridge though few people passing over it know the reason why.

Traffic was held up in another bridge while attendants captured a panther that had escaped when a circus wagon struck one of the rafters and upset its cage. For years after, people hurried through it, for the legend was that the panther never was caught and it still lay in wait within the bridge. The bridge was referred to as the Panther Bridge and business decreased so, particularly after dark, that the bridge owner painted his own name on the portals and called it Old Johnson's Bridge. The romance of covered bridge names is rich in anecdote, much of which has been forgotten; you will find names such as Noah's Ark, Joy Bride Bridge, and Tweetsie Bridge. "Tweetsie" was an obvious nickname for the Tennessee and Western, North Carolina Railroad—T.W.N.C.—which ran a narrow-gage track over the bridge. Such names, when tracked down, unveil a history and a humor typical of the times past.

When a cigarette company recently put the picture of an imaginary covered bridge on its cigarette carton and followed it up with publicity and a song called "The Kissing Bridge," any inaccuracies in the picture, such as the absence of any truss at all, were more than made up for by creating new interest in covered bridges for the people of America. Actually there was only one bridge called The Kissing Bridge for they were all kissing bridges in the sense that one was supposed to be entitled to kiss his girl while going through the darkness there. They were also all known as "wishing bridges" because any wish made while going through one was supposed to come true. The one and only Kissing Bridge, which is long gone and forgotten, was over De Voor's Mill Stream in New York City, and it crossed at the point where Fifty-Second Street now intersects Second Avenue. Yet to this day, people who are not acquainted with the country's covered bridges and think they all look alike anyway, cannot refrain from remarking about any covered bridge, saying, "Look, there is the Kissing Bridge!"

The itinerant sign-painter who traveled by wagon seldom had to pay his way across a covered bridge; there was always a sign in need of repair or a change in tolls to be lettered, and a trade in those days was never passed up. One of the first metal signs in America printed in quantity was the familiar "Walk your horses or pay two dollars fine." Timid lady drivers often paid two dollars for the privilege of hurrying through a long bridge at night and the posted fine was frequently changed to ten dollars to discourage such goings on.

The evangelists and reformers who traveled the country with a sign brush and white paint were not always content with painting their biblical mottoes on large rocks; the old barns and bridges were always under attack during an unguarded moment for they would suddenly and miraculously display such wisdom as "Prepare to meet your God," "The Wages of sin is death." When an Ohio bridge caught fire, the scene was given a comic note by the sign on its side which read "Turn or burn." Another abandoned and ruined bridge in Indiana is without any floorboards and closed to traffic; a reformer's sign across the portal still reads, "Repent for the grave lies just ahead."

No rock, fence, tree, or bridge or barn was sacred to the old-time advertising man who set out with his wagonload of posters and signs. Even outhouses, if within seeing distance from the road, received their share. In those days, paper was good and ink was thick with varnish, so many of the old posters are as colorful today as they were a hundred years ago. Thirty thousand summer suns and winter snows have decayed most of the old advertisements but those that were tacked into the snug confines of a bridge canopy or a barn shed have just weathered along with the wood, still telling you not to miss the big circus next Saturday or to use Indian Corn Cure. Many a farmer's family will still mistake an old circus poster for this year's notice and set off to see a show that folded its tents over a century ago.

A circus parade that went through a covered bridge was always an event. Coming to an agreement as to the tolls on wild animals was an almost impossible task, for animals riding in wagons were charged a different toll than those that were led across. But with the help of a friendly conference and a few free passes for the toll-taker, the parade went through except, sometimes, the elephants. Some bridges had rulings that elephants must go singly across or even ford the river elsewhere. One circus giant named Long Tom Fawcett wore for effect a stovepipe hat that made his advertised eight and a half foot height so much higher that he had to stoop to pass through; he always put his signature on the portal face of every bridge he passed through, reaching almost to the roof to do it. In later years, when he left the show, Long Tom worked for a roofer and he could nail the lower shingles in place without getting on a ladder.

A favorite during the early part of the last century were the Negro minstrels who traveled by wagon from place to place. As with the circus, one man went ahead by horse and buggy to "put up paper," that is, to advertise the coming of the show, and he too, was known as the "paper man." Scarcely a barn or covered bridge hasn't at some time or other had a minstrel poster glued to its sides. The paper man arranged rates on bridge

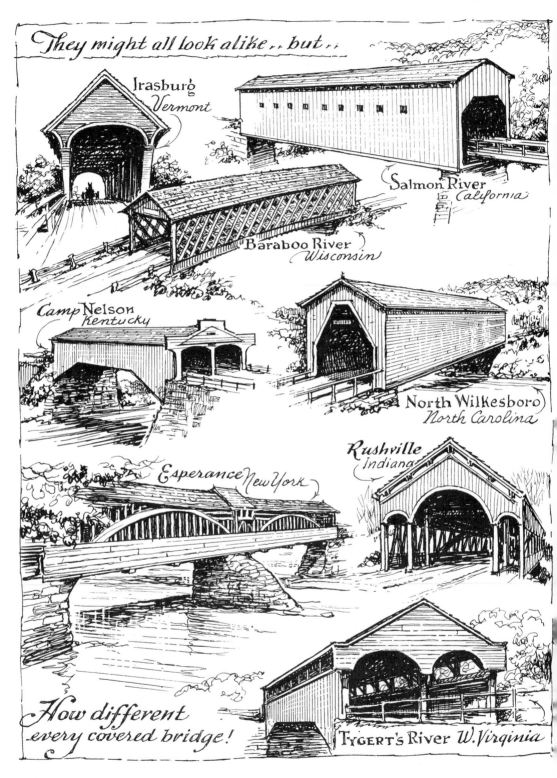

They might all look alike.. but..

Irasburg
Vermont

Salmon River
California

Baraboo River
Wisconsin

Camp Nelson
Kentucky

North Wilkesboro
North Carolina

Esperance New York

Rushville
Indiana

How different
every covered bridge!

Tygert's River W. Virginia

tolls, gave away free passes for favors and generally paved the way for a full house at the minstrel show. From all reports he was usually quite a fellow. When the town was large enough he'd often set up his stand near the covered bridge and, in blackface, with a banjo hung from his shoulders, sing and improvise his own musical announcements like the minstrels of old. It is interesting to note that Negroes have seldom, if ever, been known to play the banjo. That myth is contrived from the banjo-playing blackface minstrels who seem to have left the lasting impression with us that the early American Negro and the banjo went together.

No one liked a trade better than the Yankee peddlers; these men toured the countryside selling tinware, combs, clocks, locks, tools, and "Yankee notions." They were known never to pay cash to a bridge toll-taker but usually crossed the bridge richer than when they approached it. There was always a swap to be made in penny whistles, candy, pipes, or some sort of novelty. Many peddlers sold musical instruments and one supersalesman dressed himself in military regalia, selling applewood flutes that were made in Connecticut. Going from town to town on a white charger with saddle-bags packed full of flutes, he often sold out flutes, saddlebags, horse and all, and trudged back on foot for a new supply. All the toll-bridgekeepers in Connecticut knew him, and the best advertisement for the flutes were the well-equipped toll-keepers who had all swapped flutes for bridge passages and who all seemed to be expert flute players.

In the very beginning, it was the custom to raise bridge money by lottery, which was legalized by special acts of law wherever the church frowned upon gambling. Ready money such as was collected in tolls frequently caused trouble and some town fathers actually found difficulty in keeping down the number of bridges. One resourceful and successful bridge owner built a tavern on the other side of the bridge which, of course, meant a two-way toll for each trip to the tavern. On the other hand, there were special rates for doctors, clergymen, and large families. When it was necessary to cross a bridge to attend church, the toll-taker often gave free access, even kept shoe cloths at both ends of the bridge so that church goers could emerge dust-free. Rates varied greatly, but the tolls averaged one cent for each foot passenger and four cents for horse-drawn vehicles. "Neat creatures" [cows] were charged one cent and sheep or swine went across two for a cent. Every bridge had its sign ordering drivers to walk their horses, followed by the toll rates; but sometimes a blackboard was used and rates would be changed at will. Farmers seldom carried money with them, so charge accounts were frequent and some of the old wagons still have seat boards scratched deeply where drivers kept their own account by making a mark each time they crossed the bridge. The tolls were changed so frequently

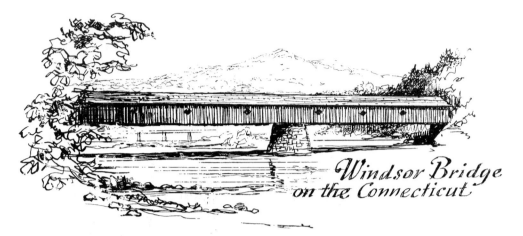

Windsor Bridge on the Connecticut

that the older signs have been redone or thrown away, but the earlier the toll sign, the more amusing is the quaint wording. One sign reads: "For each chaise, chair, sulky or other riding carriage drawn by one horse, ten cents. For each coach, chariot, phaeton or other four wheeled vehicle for passengers drawn by more than one horse, twenty cents. For each cart or other carriage of burden drawn by two beasts, ten cents and two cents for each additional oxen or pair of horses."

The toll-taker was usually a town character who could graciously take the abuse of criticism concerning the management of the bridge; others just became accustomed to it. He was always at hand for a game of checkers and he knew all the gossip and scandals of town. Many toll-takers were so often in bad favor that they spent their hours alone in knitting, a popular pastime among most bridgekeepers. The toll-taker usually kept record books, some of which are turning up to add to the romance of American history, with entries describing wolf-hunting parties, funeral processions, posses, and so on.

Despite the caution against sway and destructive vibration as might be caused by horses galloping over them, covered bridges were often used as drill halls for troops. One bridge in Alabama became a blockhouse for a troop of Union soldiers who, inside, successfully held off an enemy attack of Confederates in 1862. The large space and protection from weather made covered bridges perfect meeting places for town gatherings, particularly for meetings that the church would not accept. Lighted by candles and kerosene lamps for the secret meetings of vigilantes during peacetime and soldiers during war, covered bridges must have made rich and ghostly pictures of the time. Few of us think of covered bridges as having been lit by oil lamps, although many of them were. Wired now for electricity, the mystery of night within a covered bridge is completely blasted away with a flick of a switch. But those who look closely may see where the old lamp was hung by the countless scratchings of matches on the soft pine clapboards.

An interesting item on the record books of the bridge at Sheldon, Vermont, occurred in 1864. A group of Confederate raiders stole down across the border from Canada and robbed the bank at St. Albans, Vermont. Their plans for escape included the burning of the bridge at Sheldon, but before the bridge could be destroyed, a party of Federals caught up with the plans of the raiders and chased them through the bridge and back into Canada. Ironically, although the bridge lasted sixty-eight years more, it was destroyed by fire in 1932.

The last entry in the toll-book of Center Bridge which connected Stockton in New Jersey with the Pennsylvania shore, was on January 9, 1841. It related a hair-raising cruise by a deputy toll-collector named Fell. Down the river he sailed on a piece of his own bridge, which, along with five others, was washed away by the tremendous flood. There is no mention of why Mr. Fell was in the bridge at so precarious a moment, but the story of his trip is a thriller. After speeding for five miles in the churning water, with houses, cows, and the five other bridges to keep him company, he came to the stubbornly resisting Lambertville-New Hope bridge. His portion of bridge and private craft smashed through this, taking him merrily on toward Trenton. But at Yardley, just this side of Trenton, Mr. Fell's craft came to a halt where he disembarked, rested awhile, and took the stage the twenty miles back to his bridgeless toll-house. Here he was greeted with cheers and "a salute from a cannon."

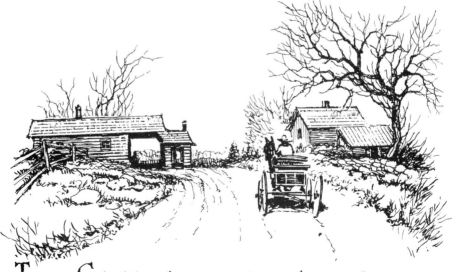

TOLL GATE *at* WINSTED, *Connecticut*

Such are the tales that keep the story of covered bridges alive, but these are also the tales that limit public interest by classifying the bridges as no more than quaint curiosities of the past. The greatness of covered bridges was their part in the public enterprise of their time and their straightforward expression of functional structure. As the barn was an expression of America in the eighteenth century, the covered bridge took over that burden for the nineteenth century.

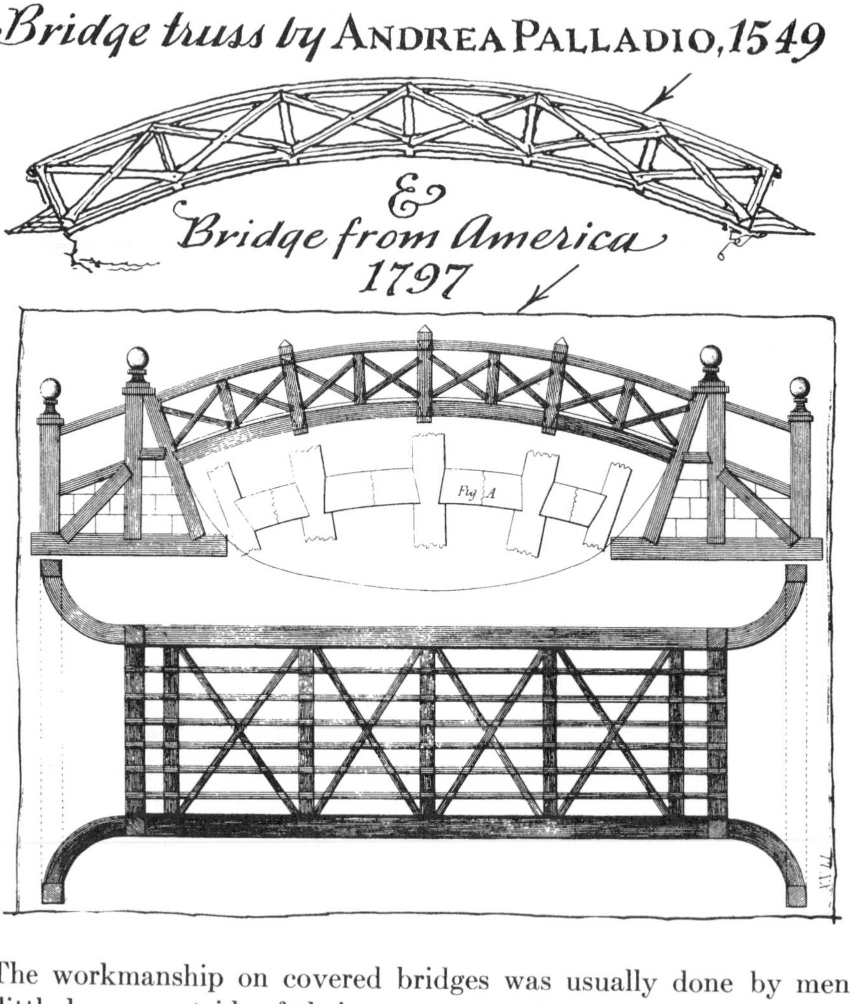

Bridge truss by ANDREA PALLADIO, *1549*

&
Bridge from America
1797

The workmanship on covered bridges was usually done by men who were little known outside of their own community and the results were more an exhibition of the small-town mastercraftsman than of the engineer. Yet the designs were those of the professional bridge-builders such as Palmer, Wernwag, Burr, Town, and others. At that time it was fashionable to try one's hand at bridge designing and many successful businessmen retired into the study of engineering with the goal of inventing a better bridge truss.

94

When a patented truss was used, the inventor received his royalty according to the length of the bridge that used his idea. Highways were becoming the lifeblood of the nation and the man who could build a better bridge was the hero of his day.

Just before the advent of the covered bridges, the American bridge-builders were trying to put architectural grace into their structures. The builders of churches were called in to design trusses and classic designs from the ancient bridges were being revived. The plan is from a 1797 handbook on building and it shows a bridge sixty feet long; the engineering is borrowed directly from Palladio. Just about this time Lewis Wernwag was beginning his career as an apprentice bridge-builder with a great urge to "put beauty back into the barnlike structures that Americans are throwing across their rivers." Using the Palladio principle, he later designed his bridge called "Colossus."

The cornerstone of the Colossus was laid in 1812 at Upper Ferry, later Fairmont, on Pennsylvania's Schuylkill River. Although its single span of three hundred and forty feet was not the longest of record, the Colossus was the most celebrated of all covered bridges until it burned down in 1838. Accounts of the Colossus conflagration describe it as "picturesque and at times, sublime": "the splendid sight," an account relates, "continued for some time, the gazers looking on in rapt silence . . . the bridge with a graceful curtsy, descended a few feet, hesitated and then with a gentle swanlike motion, sank like a dream down on the waters. But the moment the fabric touched the waves, a simmering, hissing sound was heard while ten thousand sparkles shot into the air. The moon which was just rising, appeared through the dense veil of smoke to add to the illusion." The end was in keeping with the drama of its erection and twenty-six years of fame.

The Colossus was not a typical American covered bridge at all, but its fame had kindled the spark that inspired builders throughout the country to try their hand at building the classic trusses into serviceable bridges for their own villages. There were several designs to choose from and

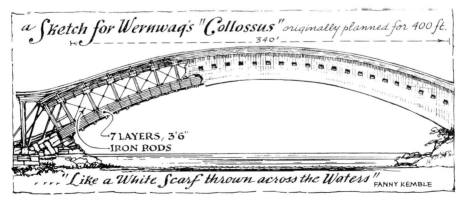

a Sketch for Wernwag's "Collossus" originally planned for 400 ft.
340'
7 LAYERS, 3'6"
IRON RODS
"Like a White Scarf thrown across the Waters" FANNY KEMBLE

The KINGPOST truss for SHORT SPANS

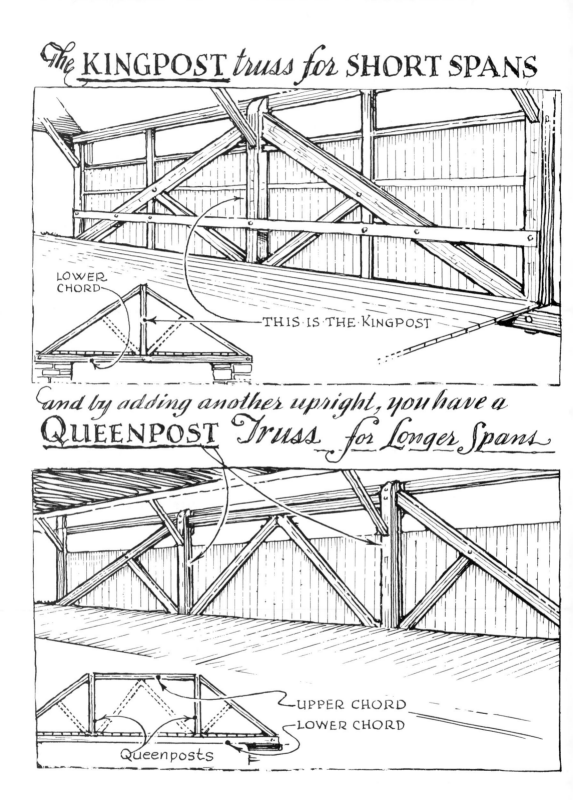

LOWER CHORD

THIS IS THE KINGPOST

and by adding another upright, you have a
QUEENPOST Truss for Longer Spans

UPPER CHORD
LOWER CHORD

Queenposts

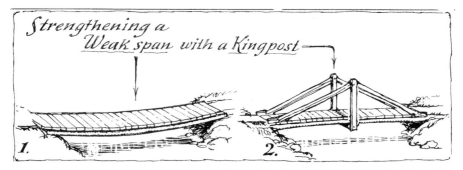

Strengthening a Weak span with a Kingpost

1.   2.

although each bore the name of an American designer or patent-holder, the ideas actually went back to ancient principles. The simplest and first truss tried in America was the kingpost truss. This consists of a center upright or kingpost in the middle of the span, with two compression pieces slanting downward and outward toward each shore. Many simple unbraced spans were later strengthened by the addition of a kingpost truss. But this arrangement was limited to small bridges because the compression pieces were limited in length. The kingpost truss shown in the bridge interior is that of Pine Brook Bridge in Waitsfield, Vermont. To make this principle adaptable to a longer bridge, two uprights are spaced across the span and the

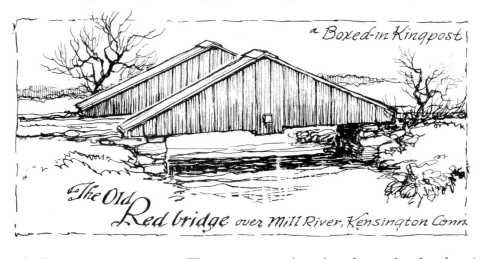

a Boxed-in Kingpost

The Old Red bridge over Mill River, Kensington Conn.

result is a queenpost truss. The queenpost interior shown in the drawing is that of a bridge at Wolcott, Vermont. The kingpost and queenpost bridges have appeared both "bare" and boxed in from the weather, and many have been covered over with a roof during later years. By using a cross instead of an inverted V in the middle of a queenpost truss, a stronger design results and this is called a Warren truss. All these simple trusses were already used in barn structure, so the barn-builder was right at home constructing small bridges.

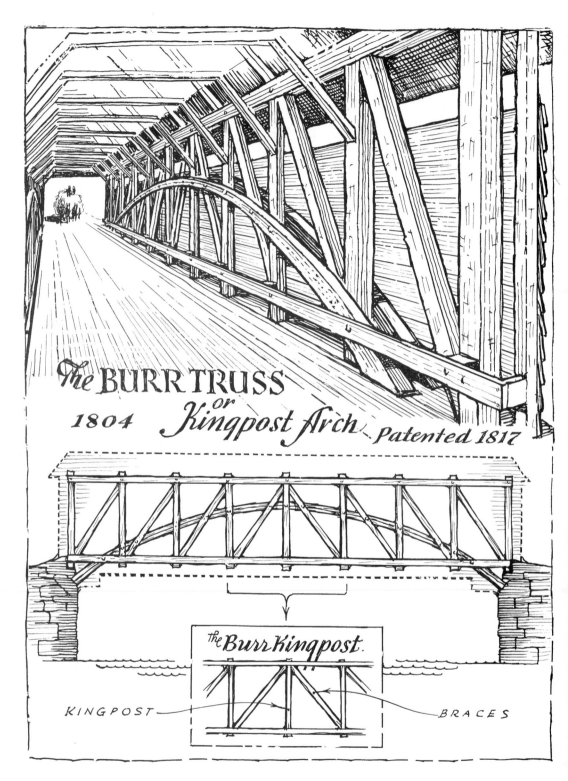

The BURR TRUSS

or

1804 Kingpost Arch Patented 1817

The Burr Kingpost.

KINGPOST — — BRACES

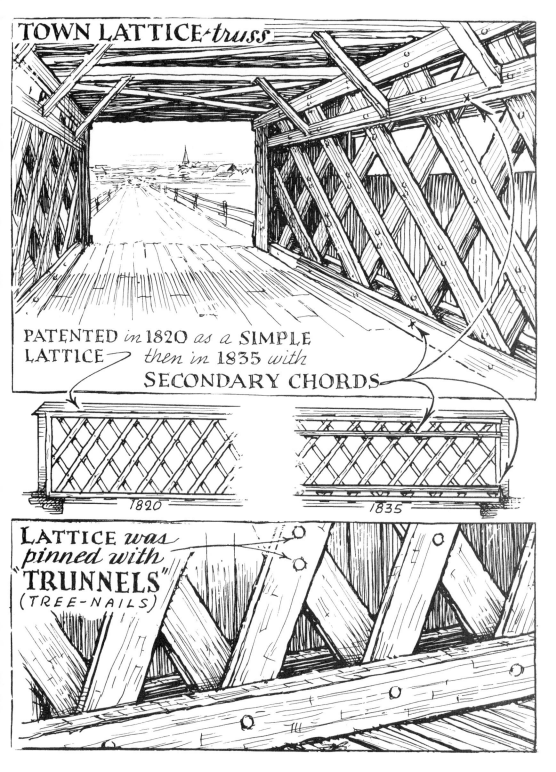

TOWN LATTICE-*truss*

PATENTED *in* 1820 *as a* SIMPLE
LATTICE ⇀ *then in* 1835 *with*
SECONDARY CHORDS

1820

1835

LATTICE *was
pinned with*
"TRUNNELS"
(TREE-NAILS)

The greatest problem of all bridge building was to make one long single arch that would still be strong. The kingpost and queenpost could not be just enlarged indefinitely. There had to be something added to strengthen them. Theodore Burr devised a series of kingposts combined with an arch. What he had in mind was to strengthen the series of kingposts with an arch but what really happened was that the arch became most important and the kingposts merely made the arch stronger. One of the first such bridges to make Burr famous was built in 1804 across the Hudson at Waterford, New York. This bridge was in prime condition up until the time it was destroyed by fire more than a hundred years later. Ironically the cause of the fire was faulty electrical connections. About thirteen years after designing it, Burr patented his Burr-arch truss. By the time Burr was forty-seven years old he had built forty-five bridges; his ideas were used or modified in countless others and many bridges were later strengthened by his arch. So many bridges are traced to Burr that he is called by many the father of American bridge building.

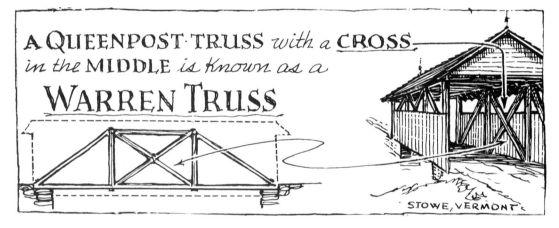

A QUEENPOST·TRUSS *with a* CROSS *in the* MIDDLE *is known as a* WARREN TRUSS

STOWE, VERMONT

Born in Thompson, Connecticut in 1784, Ithiel Town was to be another famous bridge-builder. A carpenter in his youth and an architectural student in Boston, Town built Center Church and Trinity Church on the New Haven Green while still a young man. As a bridge engineer he was granted a patent in January 1820 for his own truss. Using it in a one-hundred-foot bridge outside of New Haven, he sold rights to his patent for a dollar a foot for use in other bridges and became one of the first successful bridge-builders who could live comfortably on his royalty income. His lattice-truss may be seen in most Vermont bridges and in almost every part of the nation. In 1835 he took out a second patent for an improvement on the lattice, strengthening the arrangement with a secondary set of chords. One of the great advantages of Town's lattice-truss was that most of the bridgework

100

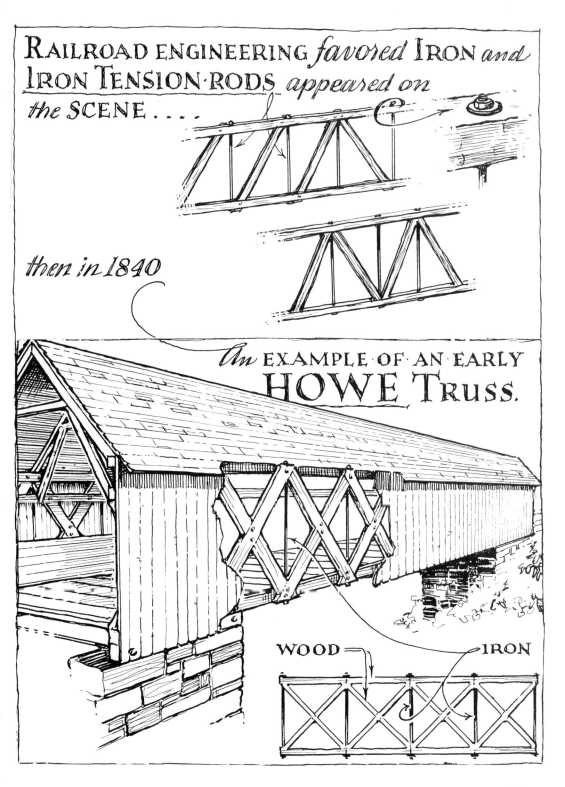

RAILROAD ENGINEERING *favored* IRON *and* IRON TENSION·RODS *appeared on* *the* SCENE. . . .

then in 1840

An EXAMPLE·OF·AN·EARLY HOWE Truss.

WOOD

IRON

could be made from shorter lengths of timber, but as time went on, the strength of the truss was also proved. The lattice design could take much abuse and an abnormal amount of weight. Town was a supersalesman and he spent much of his time traveling about the country, even to Europe, to sell his patents. He was always equipped with posters, pamphlets, and models of his bridges and although his competitors accused him of claiming patent on a design that was already in use, his fame stuck and it will endure long after the last Town lattice-truss bridge has gone.

About the time of Town's success, Colonel Stephen H. Long devised the truss that bears his name and was granted patents in 1830, 1836, and in 1839. The main feature of the Long truss was a series of crossed beams, between upright posts. Long devised his truss when he was consulting engineer for the Baltimore and Ohio Railroad, assigned by the War Department to map out that railroad's route. A short way from Baltimore the railroad was crossed by the Baltimore and Washington Turnpike and it was here that Long built his first bridge and used his X-braced panel design. But the railroads were looking for a design that used iron for bracing, and quick to realize this and to improve on Colonel Long's cross panel which the railroads already liked, William Howe of Massachusetts designed an iron and wood truss. Howe's truss featured vertical tension rods of iron. The railroads were sold and so were many of the towns which were "modernizing" with iron.

But stubborn to the idea of all-wood bridges, many designers continued devising new kinds of wooden trusses. One of the later engineers who added to the collection of bridge trusses was D. C. McCallum who patented the McCallum truss in 1851. Used mainly for railroad bridges, this truss features arched braces reaching out fanlike from the abutments (often held in place by iron "buckets") and a slightly curved upper chord. Looking at the drawing it will be seen that the complicated structural assembly made it a difficult bridge for the amateur to build and the McCallum Inflexible Arched Truss reached an early obsolescence.

In building a bridge, the exact design of the truss was not always copied and there was always a bit of legal work and discussion between the builder and the patent-holder, before the bridge went up. Very often the bridge site became a "proving ground" for the bridge or for sections of the bridge before it was finally assembled and put out over the water. The timbers were fitted on the ground and then taken apart again to be placed during the "raising" in the same manner that barn timbers were fitted, marked, and put together again during the "raisin' day."

In laying the bridge out first on land, it was never made level but had a very slight arch or camber to it. This was to take care of any sag when

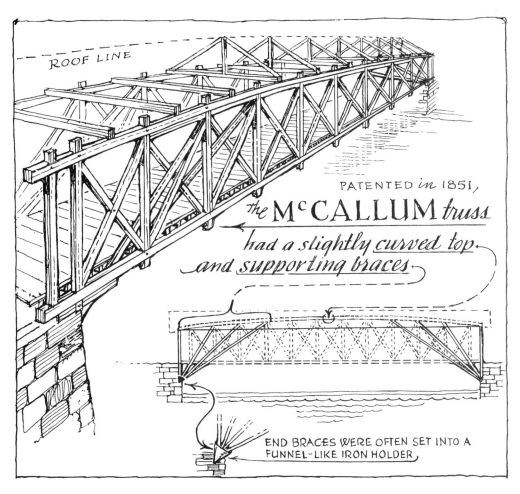

ROOF LINE

PATENTED *in 1851,*

the McCALLUM *truss*

had a slightly __curved top__
and __supporting braces__

END BRACES WERE OFTEN SET INTO A
FUNNEL-LIKE IRON HOLDER,

its own weight "set it to place." The amount of camber used was one of the builder's skills for only he could add together his own inaccuracies along with the softness or shrinkage of the wood used and estimate exactly how much differential there would be when the structure was on its own. Although the building was usually done by local men, a few builders rose to fame as bridge experts and were asked to do "outside jobs" of bridge building. One of these was Nicholas Powers. His first bridge was built at Pittsford Mills, Vermont in 1837; it was one hundred and thirty feet long and close to thirty feet wide. Nicholas was only twenty-one years old then, but his bridge still had life in it when it was torn down ninety-four years later. One of the most famous bridges that Powers built was the one at North Blenheim in New York. Put up in 1855, it has a single span of a hundred and twenty-eight feet. Powers said, "If the bridge goes down when we knock the trestle out from under it, I never want to see the sun rise again." And to prove it he sat in the middle with his legs dangling when the last chocks were knocked out. It sagged only a fraction of an inch and right on the dot to where he had predicted. They say that when an ardent prohibitionist town official came to inspect the bridge building, a jug of whiskey was hidden in the stone abutments and it is still hiding there, as the builder said, "like an alcoholic cornerstone."

Most of the remaining covered bridges are well posted with signs giving the maximum amount of weight allowed to cross their spans. Actually, this is done with all small bridges, but in these days of rough and fast driving, the heavily laden trucks are one of the things that endanger the last years of the old wooden bridges. The last covered bridge standing in the province of Ontario, at West Montrose, is posted for only two tons which was plenty for the loads of hay it was designed for. But the local school bus now crosses it and the bus itself weighs that much. So, twice a day the bus unloads its human cargo on the near side, proceeds alone to the far end and waits for the school children to troop across by foot and reload. Luckily they are sheltered from rain and snow by the bridge's roof. If the bridge is gone by the time of the writing of this book, the children will miss the daily experience that their parents will cherish forever in their memories.

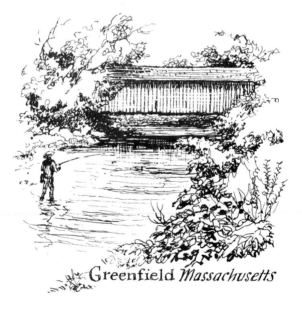

Greenfield Massachusetts

A small Gallery of Covered Bridge Types

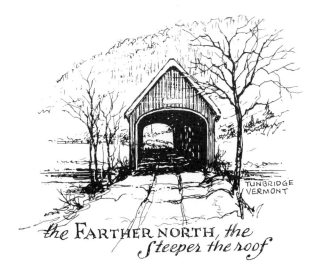

TUNBRIDGE VERMONT

the FARTHER NORTH, the steeper the roof

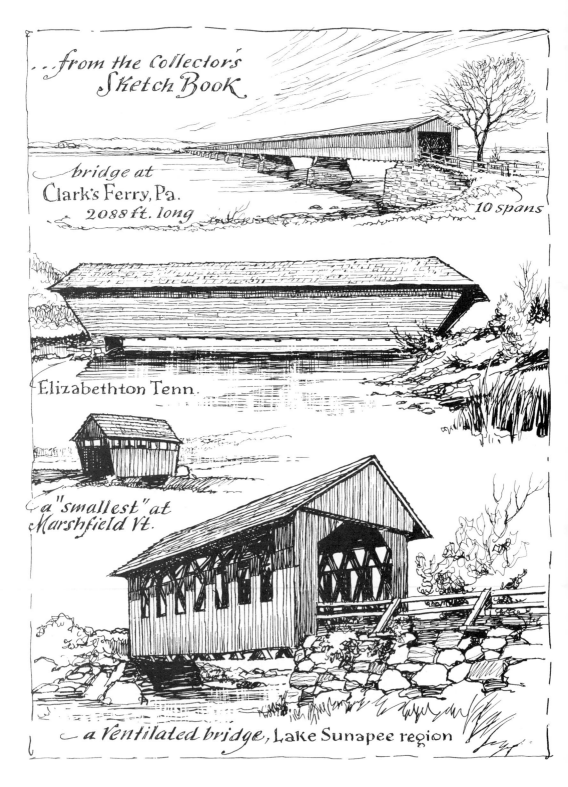

...from the Collector's
Sketch Book

bridge at
Clark's Ferry, Pa.
2088 ft. long

10 spans

Elizabethton Tenn.

a "smallest" at
Marshfield Vt.

a Ventilated bridge, Lake Sunapee region

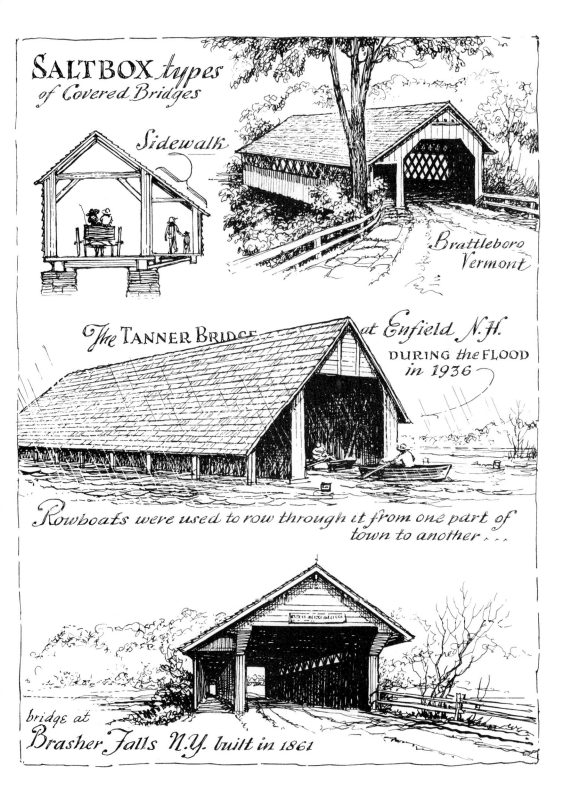

SALTBOX *types* *of Covered Bridges*

Sidewalk

Brattleboro Vermont

The TANNER BRIDGE *at Enfield N.H.* DURING *the* FLOOD *in 1936*

Rowboats were used to row through it from one part of town to another...

bridge at Brasher Falls N.Y. built in 1861

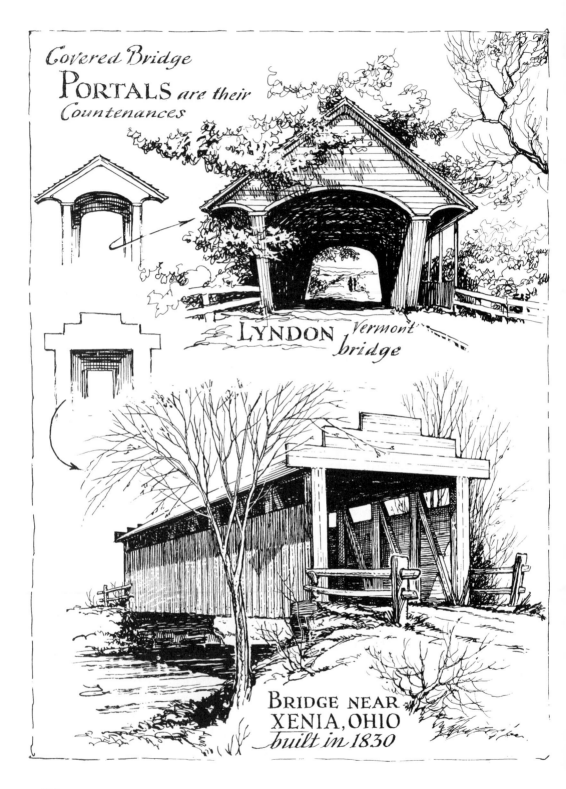

Covered Bridge
PORTALS are their
Countenances

LYNDON Vermont bridge

BRIDGE NEAR
XENIA, OHIO
built in 1830

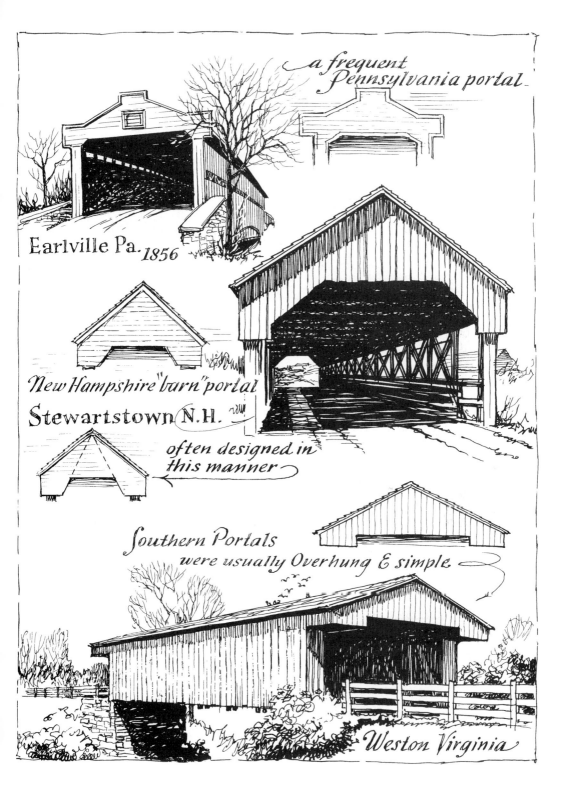

a frequent
Pennsylvania portal

Earlville Pa. 1856

New Hampshire "barn" portal
Stewartstown N.H.

often designed in
this manner

Southern Portals
were usually Overhung & simple

Weston Virginia

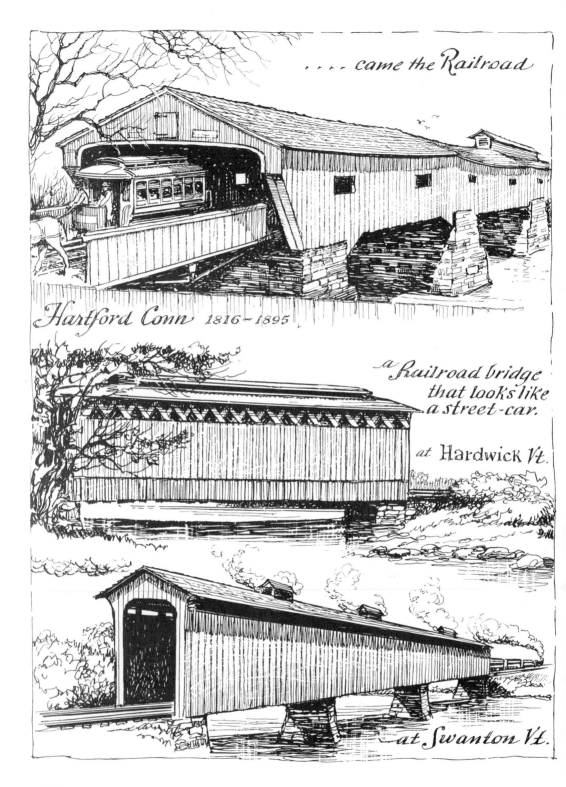

.... came the Railroad

Hartford Conn 1816-1895

a Railroad bridge
that looks like
a street-car.

at Hardwick Vt.

at Swanton Vt.

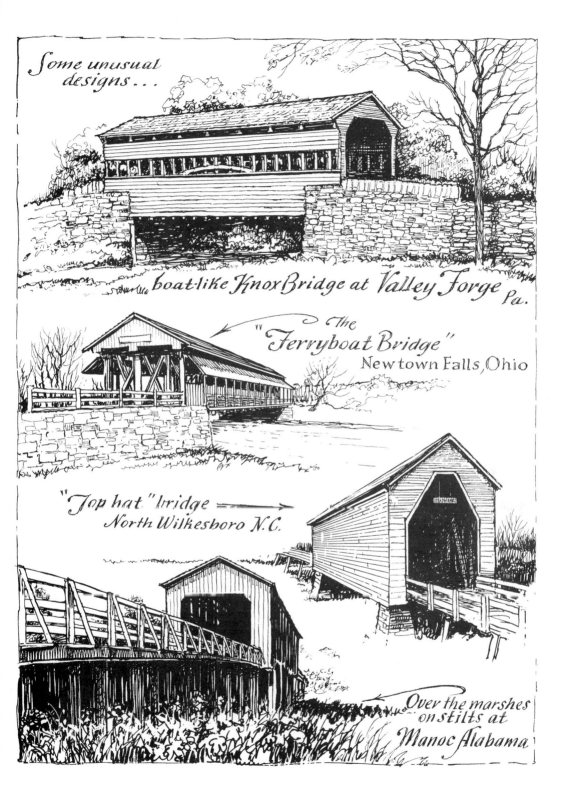

Some unusual designs...

boat-like Knox Bridge at Valley Forge Pa.

The "Ferryboat Bridge" Newtown Falls, Ohio

"Top hat" bridge North Wilkesboro N.C.

Over the marshes on stilts at Manoc Alabama

A CENSUS OF COVERED BRIDGES

EVERY DISCUSSION about covered bridges sooner or later comes around to the questions: "How many covered bridges still exist?" and "What State has the most of them?" These questions are virtually impossible of answer with any finality, for so many factors are involved. Some months may pass without the loss of a single bridge while, within a week, two or three might be destroyed by fire or by the march of state highway building. Also, many bridges are forgotten ruins—should they be counted, too?

The census below, made by Richard Sanders Allen of Round Lake, New York, is the result of many trips up and down the land, aided by much painstaking research into many local records and traditions. Figures for a few of the states are of necessity only approximate, but in most cases the list is definitive.

I am most grateful to Mr. Allen for permission to end my book with his—

Census of Covered Bridges in the United States
during the summer of 1954

State	Count	State	Count
Alabama	60	New Hampshire	54
California	16	New Jersey	1
Connecticut	3	New York	33
Delaware	4	North Carolina	3
Georgia	50	Ohio	349
Illinois	10	Oregon	149
Indiana	174	Pennsylvania	390
Iowa	13	South Carolina	5
Kansas	1	Tennessee	5
Kentucky	35	Vermont	121
Louisiana	1	Virginia	8
Maine	11	Washington	7
Maryland	8	West Virginia	52
Massachusetts	12	Wisconsin	1
Michigan	6		
Mississippi	1	Railroads	26
Missouri	8		
		TOTAL	1617